VEGETARIAN
SOUPS

VEGETARIAN
SOUPS

70 fresh and wholesome recipes, from hearty main-meal ideas to light and refreshing dishes, shown step-by-step in over 250 photographs

Consultant Editor: Anne Sheasby

southwater

This edition is published by Southwater, an imprint of Anness Publishing Ltd, Hermes House, 88–89 Blackfriars Road, London SE1 8HA; tel. 020 7401 2077; fax 020 7633 9499

www.southwaterbooks.com; www.annesspublishing.com

If you like the images in this book and would like to investigate using them for publishing, promotions or advertising, please visit our website www.practicalpictures.com for more information.

© Anness Publishing Ltd 2006, 2008

UK agent: The Manning Partnership Ltd; tel. 01225 478444; fax 01225 478440; sales@manning-partnership.co.uk

UK distributor: Grantham Book Services Ltd; tel. 01476 541080; fax 01476 541061; orders@gbs.tbs-ltd.co.uk

North American agent/distributor: National Book Network; tel. 301 459 3366; fax 301 429 5746; www.nbnbooks.com

Australian agent/distributor: Pan Macmillan Australia; tel. 1300 135 113; fax 1300 135 103; customer.service@macmillan.com.au

New Zealand agent/distributor: David Bateman Ltd; tel. (09) 415 7664; fax (09) 415 8892

A CIP catalogue record for this book is available from the British Library.

Publisher: Joanna Lorenz
Editorial Director: Judith Simons
Editors: Felicity Forster and Molly Perham
Designer: Nigel Partridge
Cover Design: Bally Design Associates
Production Controller: Pedro Nelson
Editorial Reader: Rosanna Fairhead

Material in this book was previously published in *The New Book of Soups*

ETHICAL TRADING POLICY

Because of our ongoing ecological investment programme, you, as our customer, can have the pleasure and reassurance of knowing that a tree is being cultivated on your behalf to naturally replace the materials used to make the book you are holding. For further information about this scheme, go to www.annesspublishing.com/trees

NOTES

Bracketed terms are intended for American readers.

For all recipes, quantities are given in both metric and imperial measures and, where appropriate, in standard cups and spoons. Follow one set, but not a mixture, because they are not interchangeable.

Standard spoon and cup measures are level. 1 tsp = 5ml, 1 tbsp = 15ml, 1 cup = 250ml/8fl oz.

Australian standard tablespoons are 20ml. Australian readers should use 3 tsp in place of 1 tbsp for measuring small quantities of gelatine, flour, salt, etc.

American pints are 16fl oz/2 cups. American readers should use 20fl oz/2.5 cups in place of 1 pint when measuring liquids.

Electric oven temperatures in this book are for conventional ovens. When using a fan oven, the temperature will probably need to be reduced by about 10–20°C/20–40°F. Since ovens vary, you should check with your manufacturer's instruction book for guidance.

The nutritional analysis given for each recipe is calculated per portion (i.e. serving or item), unless otherwise stated. If the recipe gives a range, such as Serves 4–6, then the nutritional analysis will be for the smaller portion size, i.e. 6 servings. Measurements for sodium do not include salt added to taste.

Medium (US large) eggs are used unless otherwise stated.

Main front cover image shows Tuscan Cannellini Bean Soup with Cavolo Nero – for recipe, see page 77

CONTENTS

INTRODUCTION

One of the best things about soup is that you can put a selection of ingredients into a pan with some well-flavoured vegetable stock, let the mixture bubble away for a short while, and within no time at all you have created a delicious, flavourful, home-made soup with very little effort. Many soups are quick and easy to make and simply combine a few key ingredients with added flavourings, such as herbs or spices, whereas other soups – perhaps for a special occasion or a more substantial meal – may require a little more preparation.

VEGETABLES

Vegetables offer the cook an infinite number of culinary possibilities, including creating a wide range of delicious and flavourful vegetarian soups. The choice is immense, and the growing demand for organic produce has led to pesticide-free vegetables becoming widely available. They are at their most nutritious when freshly picked.

Carrots

The best carrots are not restricted to the cold winter months – summer welcomes the slender, sweet new crop, often sold with their feathery tops. Look for firm, smooth carrots – the smaller they are, the sweeter they taste. Carrots should be prepared just before use to preserve their valuable nutrients. Raw carrots, cut into thin julienne strips, make an unusual and attractive garnish.

Beetroot

Beetroot (beet) combines well with other vegetables to make colourful soups such as Sweet and Sour Cabbage, Beetroot and Tomato Borscht. You can buy and use beetroots raw or cooked. Small beetroots are sweeter and more tender than the larger ones.

Swedes

The globe-shaped swede (rutabaga) has pale orange-coloured flesh with a delicate sweet flavour. Trim off the thick peel, then treat in the same way as other root vegetables. For soups, swede is usually peeled and diced, then cooked with other vegetables and stock until tender. It may be finely chopped and used in chunky vegetable soups, or cooked with stock and other ingredients, then puréed to create a smooth soup.

Left: Parsnips are best used in the winter months and make good, hearty, warming soups.

Parsnips

These winter root vegetables have a sweet, creamy flavour and are a delicious element in many soups. Parsnips are best purchased after the first frost of the year, as the cold converts their starches into sugar, enhancing their sweetness. Scrub well before use and peel only if the skin is tough. Avoid large roots, which can be rather woody.

Jerusalem artichokes

This small, knobbly tuber has a sweet, nutty flavour. Peeling can be fiddly, although scrubbing and trimming is usually sufficient. Use in the same way as potatoes – they make good, creamy soups. Store them in the refrigerator for up to a week.

Potatoes

There are thousands of potato varieties, and many lend themselves to particular cooking methods. Main crop potatoes, such as Estima and Maris Piper, and sweet potatoes (preferably the orange-fleshed variety, which have a better flavour than the cream-fleshed type) are ideal for using in soups. Potatoes are also good (especially when mashed or puréed) as a thickener for some soups. Discard any potatoes with green patches. Vitamins and minerals are stored in, or just beneath, the skin, so it is best to use potatoes unpeeled.

Buying and storing root vegetables

Seek out bright, firm, unwrinkled root vegetables and tubers that do not have soft patches. When possible, choose organically grown produce, and buy in small quantities to ensure freshness. Store root vegetables in a cool, dark place.

Cauliflower

The cream-coloured compact florets, or curds, should be encased in large, bright green leaves. There are also varieties

Left: Carrots give soup colour and flavour.

with purple or green florets. Raw or cooked cauliflower has a mild flavour and is delicious when combined with other ingredients to make tasty soups such as Curried Cauliflower Soup or Cream of Cauliflower.

Cabbage

There are several different varieties of cabbage, and one of the best to use in soups is Savoy, which has substantial, crinkly leaves with a strong flavour. Firm red and white cabbages are also good for soups as they retain their texture.

Spinach

This dark green leaf is a superb source of cancer-fighting antioxidants. It is also rich in fibre, which can help to lower harmful levels of LDL cholesterol in the body, reducing the risk of heart disease and stroke. Spinach does contain iron but not in such a rich supply as was once thought. It also contains oxalic acid, which inhibits the absorption of iron and calcium in the body. However, eating spinach with a vitamin C-rich food will increase absorption. Spinach also contains vitamins C and B6, calcium, potassium, folate, thiamine and zinc. Spinach and other leafy green vegetables are ideal shredded and added to soups or cooked in them and then puréed to create flavourful, nutritious dishes with a lovely deep green colour, ideal for swirling cream into just before serving.

Pumpkins

These are native to America, where they are traditionally eaten at Thanksgiving. Small pumpkins have sweeter, less fibrous flesh than the larger ones. Pumpkins can be used in smooth soups such as Spicy Roasted Pumpkin with Pumpkin Crisps. Squash, such as the butternut variety, makes a good alternative to pumpkin – Roasted Garlic and Butternut Squash Soup with Tomato Salsa will awaken the taste buds.

Below: Fresh, crisp cucumbers are excellent in chilled soups.

Courgettes

The most widely available summer squash, courgettes (zucchini) have most flavour when they are small and young. Standard courgettes, as well as baby courgettes, may be used on their own or with other ingredients, such as mint and yogurt, to create delicious soups. They are a key ingredient in Greek Aubergine and Courgette Soup, served with tzatziki.

Cucumbers

The Chinese say that food should be enjoyed for its texture as well as for its flavour; cucumbers have a unique texture and a refreshing, cool taste. Varieties include English cucumbers, ridged cucumbers, gherkins and kirbys. Cucumbers are ideal for chilled soups such as Gazpacho with Avocado Salsa.

Corn

There are several varieties of corn, such as the kind we eat on the cob. Baby corn cobs are picked when immature and are cooked and eaten whole. Corn and baby corn, as well as canned or frozen corn kernels, are all used in soup recipes such as Corn and Potato Chowder or Corn and Red Chilli Chowder.

Fennel

Florence fennel is closely related to the herb and spice of the same name. The short, fat bulbs have a similar texture to celery and are topped wtih edible feathery fronds. Fennel has a mild aniseed flavour, which is most potent when eaten raw. Cooking tempers the flavour, giving it a delicious sweetness, as in Potato and Fennel Soup.

Tomatoes

There are dozens of varieties of tomatoes to choose from, which vary in colour, shape and size. The egg-shaped plum tomato is perfect for many types of cooking, including soups, as it has a rich flavour and a high proportion of flesh to seeds – but it must be used when fully ripe. Too often, store-bought tomatoes are bland and tasteless because they have been picked too young. Vine-ripened and cherry tomatoes, together with large beefsteak tomatoes, have good flavour and are also good for soups.

Left: Cauliflower is good for smooth and creamy soups.

Sun-dried tomatoes add a rich intensity to soups. Genetically engineered tomatoes are now sold in some countries; check the label if this concerns you. If tomatoes are cooked with their skins on, you will find that the soup may need puréeing and straining to remove skins and seeds.

Buying and storing tomatoes

When buying tomatoes, look for deep-red fruit with a firm, yielding flesh. Tomatoes that are grown and sold locally will have the best flavour. Farmers' markets are a good place to buy vegetables, or you could grow your own. To improve the flavour of a slightly hard tomato, leave it to ripen fully at room temperature.

Peppers

In spite of their name, (bell) peppers have nothing to do with the spice pepper used as a seasoning. They are actually members of the capsicum family and are called sweet peppers, bell peppers and even bull-nose peppers. The colour of the pepper tells you something about its flavour. Green peppers are the least mature and have a fresh "raw" flavour. Red peppers are ripened green peppers and are distinctly sweeter. Yellow/orange peppers taste more or less like the red ones, although perhaps slightly less sweet. Peppers add a lovely flavour and colour to soups such as Gazpacho.

Chillies

Native to America, this member of the capsicum family is extensively used in many cuisines, including Mexican, Indian, Thai, South American and African. There are more than 200 different varieties, and they add a fiery spiciness to soups.

Avocados

Strictly a fruit rather than a vegetable, the avocado has been known by many names – butter pear and alligator pear to name but two. There are four varieties: Hass, the purple-black small bumpy avocado, the Ettinger and Fuerte, which are pear-shaped and have smooth green skin, and the Nabal, which is rounder in shape. The black-coloured Hass avocado has golden-yellow flesh, while green avocados have pale green to yellow flesh. Avocados can be used to make tempting soups such as Avocado and Lime Soup with a Green Chilli Salsa.

Above: Puréed avocados make soups really creamy.

Aubergines

The dark-purple, glossy-skinned aubergine (eggplant) is the most familiar variety, although it is the small, ivory-white egg-shaped variety that has inspired its American name. There is also the bright-green pea aubergine that is used in Asian cooking, and a pale-purple Chinese aubergine. Creamy Aubergine Soup with Mozzarella and Gremolata is delicious and will impress your dinner party guests.

Onions

Onions are an essential flavouring, offering a range of taste sensations, from the sweet and juicy red onion and powerfully pungent white onion to the light and fresh spring onion (scallion). Pearl onions and shallots are the babies of the family. Shallots and leeks can be used in place of onions in many recipes, while spring onions may be used as a flavouring or garnish.

Buying and storing onions

When buying, choose onions that have dry, papery skins and are heavy for their size. They will keep for 1–2 months in a cool, dark place.

Garlic

An ingredient that everyone who does any cooking at all will need, garlic is a bulb that is available in many varieties. Its papery skin can be white, pink or purple. Colour makes no difference to taste, but the attraction of the large purple bulbs is that they make a beautiful display in the kitchen. As a general rule, the smaller the garlic bulb, the stronger it is likely to be. Store in a cool, dry place – not in the refrigerator.

Peeling and seeding tomatoes

Tomato seeds can give soups a bitter flavour. Removing them and the tomato skins will also give a smoother result, which is preferable for many soups.

1 Immerse the tomato in boiling water and leave for about 30 seconds – the base of each tomato can be slashed to make peeling easier.

2 Lift out the tomato with a slotted spoon, rinse in cold water to cool slightly, and then peel off the skin.

3 Cut the tomato in half, then scoop out the seeds with a teaspoon and remove the hard core. Dice or coarsely chop the flesh according to the recipe.

Above: Shiitake mushrooms are popular in Japanese soups.

Leeks

Leeks have their own distinct, subtle flavour, which is less pungent than onions. Excellent in soups, they add flavour and texture. Commercially grown leeks are usually about 25cm (10in) long, but you may occasionally see baby leeks, which are very mild and tender and can also be used in soups. Try winter soups such as Irish Leek and Blue Cheese Soup.

Mushrooms

The most common cultivated variety of mushroom is actually one type in various stages of maturity. The button (white) mushroom is the youngest and has, as its name suggests, a tight, white, button-like cap. It has a mild flavour. Cap mushrooms are slightly more mature and larger in size, while the flat field (portabello) mushroom is the largest and has dark, open gills. Flat mushrooms have the most prominent flavour. Mushrooms are a useful ingredient in many soups, and add flavour and texture, as well as colour (especially the brown cap [cremini] and field mushrooms). Fresh and dried wild mushrooms also add delicious taste to soup recipes, for example in Wild Mushroom Soup with Soft Polenta.

Several varieties of wild mushroom are now available in supermarkets. Oyster mushrooms are ear-shaped fungi that grow on rotting wood. Cap, gills and stem are all the same colour, which can be greyish brown, pink or yellow. They are softer than button mushrooms when cooked but seem more substantial, having more of a "bite" to them. Shiitake mushrooms are Japanese fungi from the variety of tree mushrooms (called *take* in Japan, the *shii* being the hardwood tree from which they are harvested). They have a meaty, acid flavour and a slippery texture.

Buying and storing mushrooms

Buy mushrooms that smell and look fresh. Avoid ones with damp, slimy patches and any that are discoloured. Store in a paper bag in the refrigerator for up to 4 days. Wipe mushrooms with damp kitchen paper before use but never wash or soak them.

Rocket

Usually thought of as a salad vegetable, rocket (arugula) is actually a herb with a strong peppery taste that adds flavour and colour to soups such as Leek, Potato and Rocket Soup.

Sorrel

Another salad vegetable that is a herb, sorrel has a refreshing, sharp flavour. In soups it is good mixed with other herbs and green leaves. Salad leaves are best when they are very fresh, and do not keep well.

Above: Rocket gives soups a strong, peppery flavour.

Above: Fresh sorrel mixes well with other herbs.

Cleaning leeks

Leeks need meticulous cleaning to remove any grit and earth that may hide between the layers of leaves. This method will ensure that the very last tiny piece of grit will be washed away.

1 Trim off the root, them trim the top of the green part and discard. Remove any tough or damaged outer leaves.

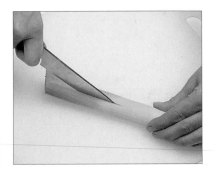

2 Slash the green part of the leek into quarters and rinse the entire leek well under cold running water, separating the layers to remove any hidden dirt or grit. Slice or leave whole, depending on the recipe.

PULSES

Low in fat and high in complex carbohydrates, vitamins and minerals, pulses – the edible seeds from plants belonging to the legume family – are an important source of protein for vegetarians.For the cook, their ability to absorb the flavours of other foods means that they are ideal in soups.

Red kidney beans

These are dark red-brown kidney-shaped beans that keep their shape and colour when cooked. They are excellent in soups as well as many other dishes. Raw kidney beans contain a substance that cannot be digested and that may cause food poisoning if the toxins are not extracted. It is therefore essential that you fast-boil red kidney beans for 15 minutes before use.

Broad beans

Usually eaten in their fresh form, broad (fava) beans change in colour from green to brown when dried, making them difficult to recognize. The outer skin can be very tough and chewy, and some people prefer to remove it after cooking. Broad beans add delicious flavour to soups – try Broad Bean, Minestrone or Catalan Potato and Broad Bean Soup.

Above: Dried broad beans can be used when fresh ones are not in season.

Cannellini beans

These small, white, kidney-shaped beans, which are sometimes called white kidney beans, have a soft, creamy texture when cooked and are popular in Italian cooking. They can be used in place of haricot (navy) beans and make a tasty addition to recipes such as Pasta, Bean and Vegetable Soup.

Chickpeas

Also known as garbanzo beans, robust and hearty chickpeas have a delicious nutty flavour and creamy texture. They need lengthy cooking and are often used in Middle Eastern cooking, in dishes such as North African Spiced Soup.

Buying and storing beans

Look for plump, shiny beans with unbroken skins. Beans toughen with age so, although they will keep for up to a year in a cool, dry place, it is best to buy small quantities from stores with a regular turnover of stock. Store in an airtight container in a cool, dark and dry place.

Left: Cannellini beans give soups a velvety and creamy texture, as well as extra fibre.

LENTILS AND PEAS

These are among our oldest foods. Lentils are hard even when fresh, so they are always sold dried. Unlike other pulses, they do not need soaking.

Red lentils

Bright orange-coloured red split lentils, sometimes known as Egyptian lentils, are the most familiar variety. They cook in just 20 minutes, disintegrating into a thick purée, and are ideal for thickening soups. Try creative recipes such as Thai-style Lentil and Coconut Soup, or Spiced Lentil Soup with Parsley Cream.

Green and brown lentils

Sometimes referred to as continental lentils, these pulses retain their disc shape when cooked. They take longer to cook than split lentils – about 40–45 minutes – and are ideal for adding to warming soups.

Peas

Dried peas come from the field pea, not the garden pea, which is eaten fresh. Unlike lentils, peas are soft when young and require drying. They are available whole or split; the latter have a sweeter flavour and cook more quickly. Like split lentils, split peas do not hold their shape when cooked, making them perfect for soups. They take about 45 minutes to cook. Dried peas require soaking overnight before use.

Buying and storing lentils and peas

Although lentils and peas can be kept for up to a year, they toughen with time. Buy from stores with a fast turnover of stock and store in airtight containers in a cool, dark place.

PASTA

Low in fat and a good source of carbohydrate, small pasta shapes such as stellete or pastina are ideal for adding to vegetarian soups. The quality of pasta varies tremendously – choose good-quality Italian brands made from 100 per cent durum wheat, and if possible buy fresh pasta from an Italian delicatessen rather than pre-packed fresh pasta from the supermarket.

Buying and storing soup pasta

Dried pasta will keep almost indefinitely in the store cupboard, but if you keep it in a storage jar, it is a good idea to use it all up before adding any from a new packet. Fresh pasta is usually sold loose and is best cooked the same day, but can be kept in the refrigerator for a day or two. Fresh pasta from a supermarket is likely to be packed in plastic packs and bags and will keep for 3–4 days in the refrigerator. Fresh pasta freezes well and should be cooked from frozen. Convenient packs of supermarket pasta have the advantage of being easy to store in the freezer.

NOODLES

Made from wheat flour, rice, mung bean flour or buckwheat flour, noodles can be used in a variety of soup recipes. Try Thai Cellophane Noodle Soup, or Udon Noodles with Egg Broth and Ginger.

Wheat noodles

These are available in two types: plain and egg. Plain noodles are made from strong flour and water; they can be flat or round and come in various thicknesses. Egg noodles are more common than the plain variety, and are sold both fresh and dried. The Chinese types are available in various thicknesses. Very fine egg noodles, which

Above:
Egg noodles add flavour and texture to soups.

resemble vermicelli, are usually sold in individual coils. More substantial wholewheat egg noodles are widely available from larger supermarkets.

Udon and ramen are types of Japanese noodles. Udon noodles are thick and can be round or flat. They are available fresh, pre-cooked or dried. Wholewheat udon noodles have a more robust flavour. Ramen egg noodles are sold in coils and in Japan they are often cooked and served with an accompanying broth.

Cellophane noodles

Made from mung beans, cellophane noodles are translucent and do not need to be boiled; they are simply soaked in boiling water for 10–15 minutes. They have a fantastic texture, which they retain when cooked, never becoming soggy.

Rice noodles

These very fine, delicate noodles are made from rice and are opaque-white in colour. Like wheat noodles, they come in various widths, from the very thin strands known as rice vermicelli, which are popular in Thailand and southern China, to the thicker rice sticks, which are used more in Vietnam and Malaysia.

Rice noodles, above, and cellophane noodles, below.

Buying and storing noodles

Dried noodles are readily available in supermarkets. Packets of fresh noodles are found in the chiller cabinets of Asian stores and some supermarkets. They must be stored in the refrigerator or freezer. Dried noodles will keep for many months in an airtight container in a cool, dry place.

HERBS

Herbs can make a significant difference to the flavour and aroma of a soup, and they can enliven the simplest of dishes.

Basil

This aromatic herb is widely used in Italian and Thai cooking. The leaves bruise easily, so are best used whole or torn, rather than cut with a knife.

Bay

These dark-green, glossy leaves are best left to dry for a few days before use. They have a robust, spicy flavour and are an essential ingredient in home-made stocks and for a bouquet garni.

Coriander

Warm and spicy, coriander (cilantro) looks similar to flat leaf parsley but its taste is completely different.

Mint

Mint has deep green leaves with a tangy scent and flavour. It is used in recipes such as Iced Melon Soup with Sorbet.

Oregano

This is a wild variety of marjoram with a robust flavour. It goes well with tomato-based soups.

Right: Basil is an important herb in Italian cooking.

Parsley

There are two types of parsley: flat leaf and curly. Both taste relatively similar, but the flat leaf variety is preferable in cooked dishes. Parsley is an excellent source of vitamin C, iron and calcium.

Thyme

This robustly flavoured aromatic herb is good in tomato-based soups, as well as soups containing lentils and beans. It is also an essential ingredient in a classic bouquet garni.

Buying and storing herbs

Fresh herbs are widely available, sold loose, in packets or growing in pots. Place stems in a jar half-filled with water and cover with a plastic bag. Sealed with an elastic band, the herbs should keep for about a week.

SPICES

Highly revered for thousands of years, spices add flavour, colour and interest to the most unassuming of ingredients, while the evocative aroma of spices stimulates the appetite.

Chillies

Chillies are available fresh as well as in dried, powdered and flaked form. Dried chillies tend to be hotter than fresh, and this is certainly true of chilli flakes, which contain both the seeds and the flesh. All types of chilli may be used in soup recipes.

Coriander

Coriander seeds have a sweet, earthy, burnt-orange flavour that is more pronounced than the fresh leaves. The ready-ground powder rapidly loses its flavour and aroma, so it is best to buy whole seeds, which are easily ground in a mortar using a pestle, or in a coffee grinder. Before grinding, lightly dry-roast the seeds to enhance the flavour.

Left: Lemon grass stalks are essential in many Asian soups.

Cumin

Cumin seeds have a robust aroma and slightly bitter taste, which is tempered by dry-roasting. Black cumin seeds are milder and sweeter. Ground cumin can be harsh, so it is best to buy the whole seeds and grind them just before use to be sure of a fresh flavour.

Ginger

Fresh root ginger is spicy, peppery and fragrant, and adds a hot, yet refreshing, flavour to soups. Choose firm, thin-skinned and unblemished roots and avoid withered, woody-looking roots as these are likely to be dry and fibrous.

Lemon grass

This long fibrous stalk has a fragrant citrus aroma and flavour when cut. It is often used in South-east Asian soups. To use, remove the tough, woody outer layers, trim the root, then cut off the lower 5cm (2in) and slice or pound in a mortar using a pestle.

Pepper

Undoubtedly the oldest, most widely used spice in the world, pepper is a versatile seasoning and is invaluable for soups, because it not only adds flavour of its own to a dish, but also brings out the flavour of the other ingredients.

Salt

It is usually best to leave the seasoning of stocks and soups until the last minute, just before serving. Add salt a little bit at a time, until you have the seasoned flavour you require.

Buying and storing spices

Always buy spices in small quantities from a store with a regular turnover. Store in airtight jars in a cool place.

EQUIPMENT AND TECHNIQUES

You won't need specialist equipment to try a wide range of tasty soup recipes – just some good knives and a chopping board, a good-quality heavy-based pan and utensils such as wooden spoons. One additional piece of equipment that is very useful is a food processor or blender, to enable you to purée cooked soups, if you wish. However, if you don't have one of these, many of the soups that require puréeing can simply be hand-pressed to make them smooth.

Heavy-based pan

For making soups you should choose a good-quality heavy-based pan. A good pan that conducts and holds heat well allows the vegetables to cook for longer before browning, so that they can be softened without changing colour.

Vegetable peelers

The quickest way to peel vegetables is to use a swivel peeler. A julienne peeler will cut vegetables such as carrots into thin strips for using in recipes or as an attractive garnish.

Chopping an onion

Use a small knife to trim the root end of the onion and remove the skin with the tough layer underneath. Cut the onion in half. Place the cut side down on a chopping board and use a large sharp knife to slice down through the onion without cutting through its root. Slice horizontally through the onion. Finally, cut down across all the original cuts and the onion will fall apart into fine dice.

Wooden spoon

To avoid damaging the base of the pan, use a wooden spoon to stir soups. Wood absorbs flavours, so wash and dry the spoon well after use, and don't leave it in the soup while it is cooking.

Whisk

A balloon whisk is useful when making some soups, for quickly incorporating ingredients such as cream, which could curdle, or flour mixtures that can form lumps. Steady the pan or bowl with one hand and, holding the whisk in the other, make quick flicking movements.

Wooden mushroom

A wooden mushroom (or champignon) is useful for pressing ingredients through a fine sieve (strainer) to make a smooth purée. The back of a large spoon or ladle can also be used.

Blender

A hand-held blender allows you to blend the soup directly in the pan. Controlling the speed is easy, to give the required consistency. Be careful not to let the blender touch the base or sides of the pan as it will damage the surface.

Mouli-legume

A more traditional tool is a mouli-legume, a cooking instrument from France that is a cross between a sieve (strainer) and a food mill. It sits over a bowl and has a blade to press the food through two fine sieves. The blade is turned by hand to push the soup through the sieves, leaving all the fibres and solids behind. A mouli-legume can grind food quickly into a coarse or fine texture.

Electric food processor and blender

The most common items of equipment for puréeing soups are food processors and free-standing blenders. Both types of machine are quick and efficient, but the food processor does not produce as smooth a result as a conventional blender, and for some recipes the soup will need to be strained afterwards. Food processors can also be used for finely chopping and slicing vegetables for salsas and garnishes.

Vegetable stock

Use this versatile stock as the basis for all vegetarian soups. It may also be used for meat, poultry or fish soups.

MAKES 2.5 LITRES/4½ PINTS/10 CUPS

INGREDIENTS
  2 leeks, roughly chopped
  3 celery sticks, roughly chopped
  1 large onion, unpeeled, roughly chopped
  2 pieces fresh root ginger, chopped
  1 yellow (bell) pepper, chopped
  1 parsnip, chopped
  mushroom stalks
  tomato peelings
  45ml/3 tbsp light soy sauce
  3 bay leaves
  a bunch of parsley stalks
  3 sprigs of fresh thyme
  1 sprig of fresh rosemary
  10ml/2 tsp salt
  freshly ground black pepper
  3.5 litres/6 pints/15 cups cold water

1 Put all the ingredients into a stockpot or large pan. Bring slowly to the boil, then lower the heat and simmer for 30 minutes, stirring from time to time.

2 Allow to cool. Strain, then discard the vegetables. The stock is ready to use.

LIGHT AND REFRESHING SOUPS

What could be a nicer way of starting a meal on a warm summer evening than a bowl of refreshing soup, served al fresco *with a bottle of chilled white wine? In this section there are some delicious chilled soups, such as Gazpacho with Avocado Salsa, Chilled Garlic and Almond Soup with Grapes, and Spiced Mango Soup with Yogurt. Or you could try a light and refreshing warm broth, for example Japanese Miso Broth with Spring Onions and Tofu, or Thai Hot and Sour Soup.*

CHILLED GARLIC AND ALMOND SOUP WITH GRAPES

THIS CREAMY CHILLED SUMMER SOUP IS BASED ON AN ANCIENT MOORISH RECIPE FROM ANDALUSIA IN SOUTHERN SPAIN. ALMONDS AND PINE NUTS ARE TYPICAL INGREDIENTS OF THIS REGION.

SERVES 6

INGREDIENTS
75g/3oz/¾ cup blanched almonds
50g/2oz/½ cup pine nuts
6 large garlic cloves, peeled
200g/7oz good-quality day-old bread,
  crusts removed
900ml–1 litre/1½–1¾ pints/3¾–4 cups
  still mineral water, chilled
120ml/4fl oz/½ cup extra virgin olive
  oil, plus extra to serve
15ml/1 tbsp sherry vinegar
30–45ml/2–3 tbsp dry sherry
250g/9oz grapes, peeled, halved
  and seeded
salt and ground white pepper
ice cubes and chopped fresh chives,
  to garnish

1 Roast the almonds and pine nuts together in a dry pan over a moderate heat until they are very lightly browned. Cool, then grind to a powder.

2 Blanch the garlic in boiling water for 3 minutes. Drain and rinse.

3 Soak the bread in 300ml/½ pint/1¼ cups of the water for 10 minutes, then squeeze dry. Process the garlic, bread, nuts and 5ml/1 tsp salt in a food processor or blender until they form a paste.

4 Gradually blend in the olive oil and sherry vinegar, followed by sufficient water to make a smooth soup with a creamy consistency.

5 Stir in 30ml/2 tbsp of the sherry. Adjust the seasoning and add more dry sherry to taste. Chill for at least 3 hours, then adjust the seasoning again and stir in a little more chilled water if the soup has thickened. Reserve a few grapes for the garnish and stir the remainder into the soup.

6 Ladle the soup into bowls (glass bowls look particularly good) and garnish with ice cubes, the reserved grapes and chopped fresh chives. Serve with additional extra virgin olive oil to drizzle over the soup to taste just before it is eaten.

COOK'S TIPS
• Toasting the nuts slightly accentuates their flavour, but you can omit this step if you prefer a paler soup.
• Blanching the garlic softens its flavour.

Energy 380Kcal/1582kJ; Protein 7g; Carbohydrate 26.1g, of which sugars 8.4g; Fat 27.3g, of which saturates 3g; Cholesterol 0mg; Calcium 83mg; Fibre 2.2g; Sodium 150mg.

GAZPACHO WITH AVOCADO SALSA

TOMATOES, CUCUMBER AND PEPPERS FORM THE BASIS OF THIS CLASSIC CHILLED SOUP. ADD A SPOONFUL OF CHUNKY, FRESH AVOCADO SALSA AND A SCATTERING OF CROÛTONS, AND SERVE FOR A LIGHT LUNCH OR SIMPLE SUPPER ON A WARM SUMMER DAY.

SERVES 4

INGREDIENTS

2 slices day-old white bread, cubed
600ml/1 pint/2½ cups chilled water
1kg/2¼lb fresh tomatoes
1 cucumber
1 red (bell) pepper, halved, seeded
  and chopped
1 fresh green chilli, seeded
  and chopped
2 garlic cloves, chopped
30ml/2 tbsp extra virgin olive oil
juice of 1 lime and 1 lemon
a few drops of Tabasco sauce
salt and ground black pepper
8 ice cubes, to garnish
a handful of basil leaves, to garnish

For the croûtons
2 slices day-old bread,
  crusts removed
1 garlic clove, halved
15ml/1 tbsp olive oil

For the avocado salsa
1 ripe avocado
5ml/1 tsp lemon juice
2.5cm/1in piece cucumber, diced
½ red chilli, seeded and
  finely chopped

1 Place the bread in a large bowl and pour over 150ml/¼pint/⅔ cup of the water. Leave to soak for 5 minutes.

2 Meanwhile, place the tomatoes in a bowl and cover with boiling water. Leave for 30 seconds, then peel off the skin, remove the seeds and finely chop the flesh.

3 Thinly peel the cucumber, cut it in half lengthways and scoop out the seeds with a teaspoon. Discard the inner part and chop the flesh.

4 Place the bread, tomatoes, cucumber, red pepper, chilli, garlic, olive oil, citrus juices and Tabasco in a food processor or blender with the remaining 450ml/¾ pint/scant 2 cups chilled water and blend until well combined but still chunky. Season to taste and chill for 2–3 hours.

5 To make the croûtons, rub the slices of bread with the garlic clove. Cut the bread into cubes and place in a plastic bag with the olive oil. Seal the bag and shake until the bread cubes are coated with the oil.

6 Heat a large non-stick frying pan and fry the croûtons over a medium heat until crisp and golden.

7 Just before serving, make the avocado salsa. Halve the avocado, remove the stone (pit), then peel and dice. Toss the avocado in the lemon juice to prevent it from browning, then place it in a serving bowl and add the cucumber and chilli. Mix well.

8 Ladle the soup into four chilled bowls and add a couple of ice cubes to each. Top each portion with a good spoonful of avocado salsa. Garnish with the basil and sprinkle the croûtons over the top of the salsa.

Energy 278Kcal/1166kJ; Protein 6.4g; Carbohydrate 32.2g, of which sugars 12.1g; Fat 14.6g, of which saturates 2.6g; Cholesterol 0mg; Calcium 80mg; Fibre 5.1g; Sodium 209mg.

CHILLED TOMATO AND SWEET PEPPER SOUP

A RECIPE INSPIRED BY THE SPANISH GAZPACHO, WHERE RAW INGREDIENTS ARE COMBINED TO MAKE A CHILLED SOUP. IN THIS RECIPE THE INGREDIENTS ARE COOKED FIRST AND THEN CHILLED.

SERVES 4

INGREDIENTS
2 red (bell) peppers, halved
45ml/3 tbsp olive oil
1 onion, finely chopped
2 garlic cloves, crushed
675g/1½lb ripe, well-flavoured
  tomatoes
150ml/¼ pint/⅔ cup red wine
600ml/1 pint/2½ cups vegetable stock
salt and ground black pepper
chopped fresh chives, to garnish
For the croûtons
2 slices day-old white bread,
  crusts removed
60ml/4 tbsp olive oil

COOK'S TIP
Any juice that accumulates in the pan after grilling (broiling) the peppers, or in the bowl, should be stirred into the soup. It will add a delectable flavour.

1 Cut each pepper half into quarters and seed. Place skin-side up on a grill (broiler) rack and cook until the skins have charred. Transfer to a bowl and cover with a plate.

2 Heat the oil in a large pan. Add the onion and garlic, and cook until soft. Meanwhile, remove the skin from the peppers and roughly chop them. Cut the tomatoes into chunks.

3 Add the peppers and tomatoes to the pan, then cover and cook gently for 10 minutes. Add the red wine and cook for a further 5 minutes, then add the stock and salt and pepper, and simmer for 20 minutes.

4 To make the croûtons, cut the bread into cubes. Heat the oil in a small frying pan, add the bread and fry until golden. Drain on paper towels, cool, then store in an airtight box.

5 Process the soup in a blender or food processor until smooth. Pour into a clean glass or ceramic bowl and leave to cool thoroughly before chilling for at least 3 hours. When the soup is cold, season to taste.

6 Serve the soup in bowls, topped with the croûtons and garnished with chopped chives.

Energy 292Kcal/1216kJ; Protein 3.4g; Carbohydrate 18.8g, of which sugars 11.8g; Fat 20.4g, of which saturates 3g; Cholesterol 0mg; Calcium 40mg; Fibre 3.5g; Sodium 92mg.

CHILLED TOMATO AND BASIL-FLOWER SOUP

THIS IS A REALLY FRESH-TASTING SOUP, PACKED WITH THE COMPLEMENTARY FLAVOURS OF TOMATO AND BASIL, AND TOPPED WITH PRETTY PINK AND PURPLE SWEET BASIL FLOWERS.

SERVES 4

INGREDIENTS

15ml/1 tbsp olive oil
1 onion, finely chopped
1 garlic clove, crushed
600ml/1 pint/2½ cups
   vegetable stock
900g/2lb tomatoes, roughly chopped
20 fresh basil leaves
a few drops of balsamic vinegar
juice of ½ lemon
150ml/¼ pint/⅔ cup natural
   (plain) yogurt
granulated sugar and salt, to taste
For the garnish
30ml/2 tbsp natural (plain) yogurt
8 small basil leaves
10ml/2 tsp basil flowers, all green
   parts removed

COOK'S TIP
Basil flowers may be small but they certainly have a beautifully aromatic flavour and are surprisingly sweet. They can be used fresh in all sorts of ways by being added with basil leaves to tomato salads or pizza toppings, sprinkled on pastas, or used as flavourings in tomato juice. To remove the flowers from the stem, simply pull – they will come away easily. Purple-leaved basil has a pretty mauve flower, which is delicious too.

1 Heat the oil in a pan and add the finely chopped onion and garlic. Fry the onion and garlic in the oil for 2–3 minutes until soft and transparent, stirring occasionally.

2 Add 300ml/½ pint/1¼ cups of the vegetable stock and the chopped tomatoes to the pan. Bring to the boil, then lower the heat and simmer the mixture for 15 minutes. Stir it occasionally to prevent it from sticking to the base of the pan.

3 Allow the mixture to cool slightly, then transfer it to a food processor and process until smooth. Press through a sieve placed over a bowl to remove the tomato skins and seeds.

4 Return the mixture to the food processor and add the remainder of the stock, half the basil leaves, the vinegar, lemon juice and yogurt. Season with sugar and salt to taste. Process until smooth. Pour into a bowl and chill.

5 Just before serving, finely shred the remaining basil leaves and add them to the soup. Pour the chilled soup into individual bowls. Garnish with yogurt topped with a few small basil leaves and a sprinkling of basil flowers.

Energy 89Kcal/377kJ; Protein 3.7g; Carbohydrate 11g, of which sugars 10.6g; Fat 3.8g, of which saturates 0.8g; Cholesterol 1mg; Calcium 91mg; Fibre 2.5g; Sodium 52mg.

ICED MELON SOUP WITH SORBET

USE DIFFERENT MELONS FOR THE COOL SOUP AND ICE SORBET TO CREATE A SUBTLE CONTRAST IN FLAVOUR AND COLOUR. TRY A COMBINATION OF CHARENTAIS, OGEN OR CANTALOUPE.

SERVES 6–8

INGREDIENTS
    2.25kg/5–5¼lb very ripe melon
    45ml/3 tbsp orange juice
    30ml/2 tbsp lemon juice
    mint leaves, to garnish
For the sorbet (sherbet)
    25g/1oz/2 tbsp granulated
       sugar
    120ml/4fl oz/½ cup water
    2.25kg/5–5¼lb very ripe melon
    juice of 2 limes
    30ml/2 tbsp chopped fresh mint

1 To make the melon and mint sorbet, put the sugar and water into a pan and heat gently until the sugar dissolves. Bring to the boil and simmer for 4–5 minutes, then remove from the heat and leave to cool.

2 Halve the melon. Scrape out the seeds, then scoop out the flesh. Purée in a food processor or blender with the cooled syrup and lime juice.

3 Stir in the mint and pour the melon mixture into an ice-cream maker. Churn, following the manufacturer's instructions, or until the sorbet is smooth and firm. Alternatively, pour the mixture into a suitable container and freeze until icy around the edges. Transfer to a food processor or blender and process until smooth.

4 Repeat the freezing and processing two or three times or until the mixture is smooth and holding its shape, then freeze until firm.

5 To make the chilled melon soup, prepare the melon as in step 2 and purée it in a food processor or blender. Pour the purée into a bowl and stir in the orange and lemon juice. Place the soup in the refrigerator for 30–40 minutes, but do not chill it for too long as this will dull its flavour.

6 Ladle the soup into bowls and add a large scoop of the melon and mint sorbet to each. Garnish with mint leaves and serve at once.

SPICED MANGO SOUP WITH YOGURT

THIS DELICIOUS, LIGHT SOUP COMES FROM CHUTNEY MARY'S, AN ANGLO-INDIAN RESTAURANT IN LONDON. IT IS BEST WHEN SERVED LIGHTLY CHILLED.

SERVES 4

INGREDIENTS

2 ripe mangoes
15ml/1 tbsp gram flour
120ml/4fl oz/½ cup natural (plain) yogurt
900ml/1½ pints/3¾ cups cold water
2.5ml/½ tsp grated fresh root ginger
2 red chillies, seeded and finely chopped
30ml/2 tbsp olive oil
2.5ml/½ tsp mustard seeds
2.5ml/½ tsp cumin seeds
8 curry leaves
salt and ground black pepper
fresh mint leaves, shredded, to garnish
natural yogurt, to serve

1 Peel the mangoes, remove the stones and cut the flesh into chunks. Purée in a food processor or blender until smooth.

2 Pour into a pan and stir in the gram flour, yogurt, water, ginger and chillies. Bring to the boil, stirring occasionally. Simmer for 4–5 minutes until thickened slightly, then set aside off the heat.

3 Heat the oil in a frying pan. Add the mustard seeds and cook for a few seconds until they begin to pop, then add the cumin seeds.

4 Add the curry leaves and then cook for 5 minutes. Stir the spice mixture into the soup, return it to the heat and cook for 10 minutes.

5 Press through a mouli-legume or a sieve (strainer), if you like, then season to taste. Leave the soup to cool completely, then chill for at least 1 hour.

6 Ladle the soup into bowls, and top each with a dollop of yogurt. Garnish with shredded mint leaves and serve.

Energy 121Kcal/508kJ; Protein 2.8g; Carbohydrate 14.7g, of which sugars 12.7g; Fat 6.2g, of which saturates 1g; Cholesterol 0mg; Calcium 73mg; Fibre 2.4g; Sodium 28mg.

VICHYSSOISE

THIS CLASSIC, CHILLED SUMMER SOUP WAS FIRST CREATED IN THE 1920s BY LOUIS DIAT, CHEF AT THE NEW YORK RITZ-CARLTON. HE NAMED IT AFTER VICHY, NEAR HIS HOME IN FRANCE.

3 Stir in the stock or water, 5ml/1 tsp salt and pepper to taste. Bring to the boil, then reduce the heat and partly cover the pan. Simmer for 15 minutes, or until the potatoes are soft.

4 Cool, then process the soup until smooth in a blender or food processor. Strain the soup into a bowl and stir in the cream. Taste and adjust the seasoning and add a little iced water if the consistency of the soup seems too thick.

5 Chill the soup for at least 4 hours or until very cold. Taste the chilled soup for seasoning and add a squeeze of lemon juice, if required. Pour the soup into bowls and sprinkle with chopped chives. Serve immediately.

SERVES 4–6

INGREDIENTS
  50g/2oz/¼ cup unsalted butter
  450g/1lb leeks, white parts only,
    thinly sliced
  3 large shallots, sliced
  250g/9oz floury potatoes (such as
    King Edward or Maris Piper), peeled
    and cut into chunks
  1 litre/1¾ pints/4 cups light chicken
    stock or water
  300ml/½ pint/1¼ cups double
    (heavy) cream
  iced water (optional)
  a little lemon juice (optional)
  salt and ground black pepper
  chopped fresh chives,
    to garnish

1 Melt the butter in a heavy-based pan and cook the leeks and shallots gently, covered, for 15–20 minutes, until soft but not browned.

2 Add the potatoes and cook, uncovered, for a few minutes.

VARIATIONS
• **Potage Bonne Femme** For this hot leek and potato soup, use 1 chopped onion instead of the shallots and 450g/1lb potatoes. Halve the quantity of double (heavy) cream and reheat the puréed soup, adding a little milk if the soup seems very thick. Deep-fried shredded leek may be used to garnish the soup, instead of chopped fresh chives.
• **Chilled Leek and Sorrel or Watercress Soup** Add about 50g/2oz/1 cup shredded sorrel to the soup at the end of cooking. Finish and chill as in the main recipe, then serve the soup garnished with a little pile of finely shredded sorrel. The same quantity of watercress can be used in the same way.

Energy 547Kcal/2260kJ; Protein 4.6g; Carbohydrate 17.7g, of which sugars 6.8g; Fat 51.4g, of which saturates 31.7g; Cholesterol 129mg; Calcium 79mg; Fibre 3.6g; Sodium 103mg.

THAI HOT AND SOUR SOUP

THIS LIGHT AND INVIGORATING SOUP, WITH ITS FINELY BALANCED COMBINATION OF FLAVOURS,
IS BEST SERVED AT THE BEGINNING OF A MEAL TO STIMULATE THE APPETITE.

SERVES 4

INGREDIENTS

2 carrots
900ml/1½ pints/3¾ cups
  vegetable stock
2 Thai chillies, seeded and
  finely sliced
2 lemon grass stalks, outer leaves
  removed and each stalk cut into
  3 pieces
4 kaffir lime leaves
2 garlic cloves, finely chopped
4 spring onions (scallions),
  finely sliced
5ml/1 tsp sugar
juice of 1 lime
45ml/3 tbsp chopped fresh
  coriander (cilantro)
salt
130g/4½oz/1 cup Japanese
  tofu, sliced

1 To make carrot flowers, cut each
carrot in half crossways, then cut four
v-shaped channels lengthways. Slice
into thin rounds and set aside.

2 Pour the stock into a large pan.
Reserve 2.5ml/½ tsp of the chillies and
add the rest to the pan with the lemon
grass, lime leaves, garlic and half the
spring onions. Bring to the boil, reduce
the heat and simmer for 20 minutes.

3 Strain the stock and discard the
flavourings. Return the stock to the pan,
add the reserved chillies and spring
onions, the sugar, lime juice, coriander
and salt to taste.

4 Simmer over a gentle heat for
5 minutes, then add the carrot flowers
and the tofu, and cook for a further
2 minutes until the carrot is just tender.
Ladle into bowls and serve hot.

Energy 40Kcal/169kJ; Protein 3.3g; Carbohydrate 3.4g, of which sugars 3.1g; Fat 1.6g, of which saturates 0.2g; Cholesterol 0mg; Calcium 197mg; Fibre 1.2g; Sodium 11mg.

MISO BROTH WITH SPRING ONIONS AND TOFU

THE JAPANESE EAT MISO BROTH, A SIMPLE BUT HIGHLY NUTRITIOUS SOUP, ALMOST EVERY DAY — IT IS STANDARD BREAKFAST FARE AND IT IS EATEN WITH RICE OR NOODLES LATER IN THE DAY.

SERVES 4

INGREDIENTS

- 1 bunch of spring onions (scallions) or 5 baby leeks
- 15g/½oz fresh coriander (cilantro)
- 3 thin slices fresh root ginger
- 2 star anise
- 1 small dried red chilli
- 1.2 litres/2 pints/5 cups dashi stock or vegetable stock
- 225g/8oz pak choi (bok choy) or other Asian greens, thickly sliced
- 200g/7oz firm tofu, cut into 2.5cm/1in cubes
- 60ml/4 tbsp red miso
- 30–45ml/2–3 tbsp Japanese soy sauce (shoyu)
- 1 fresh red chilli, seeded and shredded (optional)

1 Cut the coarse green tops off the spring onions or baby leeks and slice the rest of the spring onions or leeks finely on the diagonal. Place the coarse green tops in a large pan with the coriander stalks, fresh root ginger, star anise, dried chilli and dashi or vegetable stock.

2 Heat the mixture gently until boiling, then lower the heat and simmer for 10 minutes. Strain, return to the pan and reheat until simmering. Add the green portion of the sliced spring onions or leeks to the soup with the pak choi or greens and tofu. Cook for 2 minutes.

3 Mix 45ml/3 tbsp of the miso with a little of the hot soup in a bowl, then stir it into the soup. Taste the soup and add more miso with soy sauce to taste.

4 Coarsely chop the coriander leaves and stir most of them into the soup with the white part of the spring onions or leeks. Cook for 1 minute, then ladle the soup into warmed serving bowls. Sprinkle with the remaining coriander and the fresh red chilli, if using, and serve at once.

COOK'S TIP
Dashi is available powdered in Asian and Chinese stores. Alternatively, make your own by gently simmering 10–15cm/ 4–6in kombu seaweed in 1.2 litres/ 2 pints/5 cups water for 10 minutes. Do not boil vigorously as this makes the dashi bitter. Remove the kombu, then add 15g/½oz dried bonito flakes and bring to the boil. Strain immediately through a fine sieve (strainer).

Energy 60Kcal/252kJ; Protein 5.5g; Carbohydrate 4.4g, of which sugars 4.1g; Fat 2.3g, of which saturates 0.3g; Cholesterol 0mg; Calcium 294mg; Fibre 1.6g; Sodium 453mg.

HOT AND SWEET VEGETABLE AND TOFU SOUP

THIS SOOTHING, NUTRITIOUS SOUP TAKES ONLY MINUTES TO MAKE AS THE SPINACH AND SILKEN TOFU ARE SIMPLY PLACED IN BOWLS AND COVERED WITH THE FLAVOURED HOT STOCK.

SERVES 4

INGREDIENTS
1.2 litres/2 pints/5 cups
  vegetable stock
5–10ml/1–2 tsp Thai red
  curry paste
2 kaffir lime leaves, torn
40g/1½oz/3 tbsp palm sugar or light
  muscovado (brown) sugar
30ml/2 tbsp soy sauce
juice of 1 lime
1 carrot, cut into thin batons
50g/2oz baby spinach leaves, any
  coarse stalks removed
225g/8oz block silken tofu, diced

1 Heat the stock in a large pan, then add the red curry paste. Stir constantly over a medium heat until the paste has dissolved. Add the lime leaves, sugar and soy sauce and bring to the boil.

2 Add the lime juice and carrot to the pan. Reduce the heat and simmer for 5–10 minutes. Place the spinach and tofu in four individual serving bowls and pour the hot stock on top to serve.

Energy 105Kcal/439kJ; Protein 5.3g; Carbohydrate 13.2g, of which sugars 12.8g; Fat 3.8g, of which saturates 0.5g; Cholesterol 0mg; Calcium 320mg; Fibre 0.7g; Sodium 559mg.

PEAR <u>AND</u> ROQUEFORT SOUP <u>WITH</u> CARAMELIZED PEARS

LIKE MOST FRUIT-BASED SOUPS, THIS IS SERVED IN SMALL PORTIONS. IT MAKES AN UNUSUAL AND SEASONAL APPETIZER FOR AN AUTUMN DINNER PARTY.

3 Cool the soup slightly and purée it in a food processor until smooth, then pass it through a fine sieve (strainer). Return the soup to the pan.

4 To make the caramelized pears, melt the butter in a frying pan and add the pears. Cook for 8–10 minutes, turning occasionally, until golden.

5 Reheat the soup gently, then ladle into small, shallow bowls and add a few caramelized pear wedges to each portion. Garnish with tiny sprigs of watercress and serve at once.

VARIATION
Any blue cheese with a strong flavour could be used in place of Roquefort, for example Stilton or Gorgonzola.

SERVES 4

INGREDIENTS
　30ml/2 tbsp sunflower oil
　1 onion, chopped
　3 pears, peeled, cored and
　　chopped into 1cm/½in chunks
　400ml/14fl oz/1⅔ cups
　　vegetable stock
　2.5ml/½ tsp paprika
　juice of ½ lemon
　175g/6oz Roquefort cheese
　salt and ground black pepper
　watercress sprigs, to garnish
For the caramelized pears
　50g/2oz/¼ cup butter
　2 pears, halved, cored and cut
　　into wedges

1 Heat the oil in a pan. Add the onion and cook for 4–5 minutes until soft.

2 Add the pears and stock. Bring to the boil and cook for 8–10 minutes, until the pears are soft. Stir in the paprika, lemon juice, cheese and seasoning.

Energy 381Kcal/1579kJ; Protein 10.1g; Carbohydrate 21.8g, of which sugars 20.9g; Fat 28.7g, of which saturates 15.6g; Cholesterol 59mg; Calcium 246mg; Fibre 4.7g; Sodium 616mg.

AVOCADO AND LIME SOUP WITH A GREEN CHILLI SALSA

INSPIRED BY GUACAMOLE, THE POPULAR AVOCADO DIP, THIS CREAMY SOUP RELIES ON GOOD-QUALITY RIPE AVOCADOS FOR ITS FLAVOUR AND COLOUR.

SERVES 4

INGREDIENTS
  3 ripe avocados
  juice of 1½ limes
  1 garlic clove, crushed
  handful of ice cubes
  400ml/14fl oz/1⅔ cups vegetable
    stock, chilled
  400ml/14fl oz/1⅔ cups milk, chilled
  150ml/¼ pint/⅔ cup soured
    cream, chilled
  few drops of Tabasco sauce
  salt and ground black pepper
  fresh coriander (cilantro) leaves,
    to garnish
  extra virgin olive oil, to serve
For the salsa
  4 tomatoes, peeled, seeded and
    finely diced
  2 spring onions (scallions), finely
    chopped
  1 green chilli, seeded and finely
    chopped
  15ml/1 tbsp chopped fresh
    coriander leaves
  juice of ½ lime

1 Prepare the salsa first. Mix all the ingredients together and season well. Chill in the refrigerator until required.

2 Halve the avocados and remove the stones (pits). Scoop the flesh out of the avocado skins using a spoon or melon baller and place in a food processor or blender. Add the lime juice, garlic, ice cubes and 150ml/¼ pint/⅔ cup of the chilled vegetable stock.

3 Process the soup until smooth. Pour into a large bowl and stir in the remaining vegetable stock, chilled milk, soured cream and Tabasco sauce. Season to taste.

COOK'S TIPS
• It is easy to remove the stone (pit) from an avocado. Halve the avocado and simply tap the stone firmly with the edge of a large knife. Twist the knife gently and the stone will pop out.
• This soup may discolour if left standing for too long, but the flavour will not be spoilt. Give the soup a quick whisk just before serving.

4 Ladle the soup into bowls or glasses and spoon a little salsa on top. Add a splash of olive oil to each portion and garnish with fresh coriander leaves. Serve immediately.

Energy 353Kcal/1463kJ; Protein 7.3g; Carbohydrate 11.1g, of which sugars 9.6g; Fat 31.2g, of which saturates 10.5g; Cholesterol 28mg; Calcium 175mg; Fibre 4.8g; Sodium 73mg.

SMOOTH VEGETABLE SOUPS

A bowl of smooth and creamy vegetable soup served with some crusty bread makes an excellent light lunch at any time of year. Choose whichever vegetables are fresh and in season — tomatoes and herbs in the summer, pumpkins and squash for the autumn, leeks and root vegetables during the winter months. In this section you will find traditional Parsnip Soup from Ireland alongside exotic dishes such as Spanish Sherried Onion and Almond Soup with Saffron.

CARROT AND ORANGE SOUP

THIS TRADITIONAL BRIGHT AND SUMMERY SOUP IS ALWAYS POPULAR FOR ITS WONDERFULLY CREAMY CONSISTENCY AND VIBRANTLY FRESH CITRUS FLAVOUR. USE A GOOD, HOME-MADE CHICKEN OR VEGETABLE STOCK IF YOU CAN, FOR THE BEST RESULTS.

SERVES 4

INGREDIENTS
   50g/2oz/¼ cup butter
   3 leeks, sliced
   450g/1lb carrots, sliced
   1.2 litres/2 pints/5 cups
     vegetable stock
   rind and juice of 2 oranges
   2.5ml/½ tsp freshly grated nutmeg
   150ml/¼ pint/⅔ cup Greek
     (US strained plain) yogurt
   salt and ground black pepper
   fresh sprigs of coriander (cilantro),
     to garnish

1 Melt the butter in a large pan. Add the leeks and carrots and stir well, coating the vegetables with the butter. Cover and cook for about 10 minutes, until the vegetables are beginning to soften but not colour.

2 Pour in the stock and the orange rind and juice. Add the nutmeg and season to taste with salt and pepper. Bring to the boil, lower the heat, cover and simmer for about 40 minutes, or until the vegetables are tender.

3 Leave to cool slightly, then purée the soup in a food processor or blender until smooth.

4 Return the soup to the pan and add 30ml/2 tbsp of the yogurt, then taste the soup and adjust the seasoning, if necessary. Reheat gently.

5 Ladle the soup into warm individual bowls and put a swirl of yogurt in the centre of each. Sprinkle the fresh sprigs of coriander over each bowl to garnish, and serve immediately.

Energy 206Kcal/856kJ; Protein 5g; Carbohydrate 15.8g, of which sugars 14.2g; Fat 14.4g, of which saturates 8.3g; Cholesterol 27mg; Calcium 111mg; Fibre 5.8g; Sodium 131mg.

PARSNIP SOUP

THIS LIGHTLY SPICED SOUP HAS BECOME VERY POPULAR IN IRELAND IN RECENT YEARS, AND MANY VARIATIONS ABOUND, INCLUDING THIS TRADITIONAL IRISH COMBINATION WHERE PARSNIP AND APPLE ARE USED IN EQUAL PROPORTIONS.

SERVES 6

INGREDIENTS
900g/2lb parsnips
50g/2oz/¼ cup butter
1 onion, chopped
2 garlic cloves, crushed
10ml/2 tsp ground cumin
5ml/1 tsp ground coriander
about 1.2 litres/2 pints/5 cups hot
  vegetable stock
150ml/¼ pint/⅔ cup single
  (light) cream
salt and ground black pepper
chopped fresh chives or parsley
  and/or croûtons, to garnish

COOK'S TIP
Parsnips taste best after the first frost as the cold converts their starches into sugar, enhancing their sweetness.

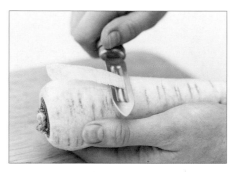

1 Peel and thinly slice the parsnips. Heat the butter in a large heavy pan and add the peeled parsnips and chopped onion with the crushed garlic. Cook until softened but not coloured, stirring occasionally. Add the ground cumin and ground coriander to the vegetable mixture and cook, stirring, for 1–2 minutes, and then gradually blend in the hot chicken stock and mix well.

2 Cover and simmer for about 20 minutes, or until the parsnip is soft. Purée the soup, adjust the texture with extra stock or water if it seems too thick, and check the seasoning. Add the cream and reheat without boiling.

3 Serve immediately, sprinkled with chopped chives or parsley and/or croûtons, to garnish.

Energy 215Kcal/899kJ; Protein 3.9g; Carbohydrate 21.3g, of which sugars 10.6g; Fat 13.3g, of which saturates 7.7g; Cholesterol 32mg; Calcium 92mg; Fibre 7.3g; Sodium 74mg.

ROASTED ROOT VEGETABLE SOUP

ROASTING THE VEGETABLES GIVES THIS WINTER SOUP A WONDERFUL DEPTH OF FLAVOUR. YOU CAN USE OTHER VEGETABLES, IF YOU WISH, OR ADAPT THE QUANTITIES DEPENDING ON WHAT'S IN SEASON.

SERVES 6

INGREDIENTS

  50ml/2fl oz/¼ cup olive oil
  1 small butternut squash, peeled,
    seeded and cubed
  2 carrots, cut into thick rounds
  1 large parsnip, cubed
  1 small swede (rutabaga), cubed
  2 leeks, thickly sliced
  1 onion, quartered
  3 bay leaves
  4 thyme sprigs, plus extra to garnish
  3 rosemary sprigs
  1.2 litres/2 pints/5 cups
    vegetable stock
salt and freshly ground black pepper
soured cream, to serve

1 Preheat the oven to 200°C/400°F/ Gas 6.

2 Pour the olive oil into a large bowl. Add the prepared vegetables and toss thoroughly with a spoon until they are all coated in the oil.

3 Spread out the vegetables in a single layer on one large or two small baking sheets. Tuck the bay leaves and the thyme and rosemary sprigs amongst the vegetables.

4 Roast the vegetables for about 50 minutes until tender, turning them occasionally to make sure they brown evenly. Remove from the oven, discard the herbs and transfer the vegetables to a large pan.

5 Pour the stock into the pan and bring to the boil. Reduce the heat, season to taste, then simmer for 10 minutes. Transfer the soup to a food processor or blender (or use a hand blender) and process for a few minutes until thick and smooth.

6 Return the soup to the pan to heat through. Season and serve with a swirl of soured cream. Garnish each serving with a sprig of thyme.

COOK'S TIP
Dried herbs can be used in place of fresh; sprinkle 2.5ml/½ tsp of each type over the vegetables in step 2 above.

Energy 65Kcal/272kJ; Protein 2.5g; Carbohydrate 11.3g, of which sugars 8.8g; Fat 1.3g, of which saturates 0.3g; Cholesterol 0mg; Calcium 93mg; Fibre 4.4g; Sodium 13mg.

LEEK, POTATO AND ROCKET SOUP

ROCKET ADDS ITS DISTINCTIVE, PEPPERY TASTE TO THIS WONDERFULLY SATISFYING SOUP.
SERVE IT HOT, GARNISHED WITH A GENEROUS SPRINKLING OF TASTY CIABATTA CROÛTONS.

SERVES 4–6

INGREDIENTS

    50g/2oz/4 tbsp butter
    1 onion, chopped
    3 leeks, chopped
    2 medium floury potatoes, diced
    900ml/1½ pints/3¾ cups vegetable
      stock or water
    2 large handfuls rocket (arugula)
    150ml/¼ pint/⅔ cup double
      (heavy) cream
    salt and ground black pepper
    garlic-flavoured ciabatta croûtons,
      to serve

1 Melt the butter in a large heavy-based pan, then add the onion, leeks and potatoes and stir until the vegetables are coated in butter. Heat the ingredients until sizzling then reduce the heat to low.

2 Cover and sweat the vegetables for 15 minutes. Pour in the stock or water and bring to the boil then reduce the heat, cover again and simmer for 20 minutes until the vegetables are tender.

3 Press the soup through a sieve (strainer) or pass through a food mill and return to the rinsed pan. (When puréeing the soup, don't use a blender or food processor, as these will give it a gluey texture.) Chop the rocket, add it to the pan and cook the soup gently, uncovered, for 5 minutes.

4 Stir in the cream, then season to taste and reheat gently. Ladle the soup into warmed soup bowls and serve with a scattering of garlic-flavoured ciabatta croûtons in each.

Energy 393Kcal/1631kJ; Protein 5.2g; Carbohydrate 23.6g, of which sugars 7.1g; Fat 31.5g, of which saturates 19.3g; Cholesterol 78mg; Calcium 87mg; Fibre 4.5g; Sodium 116mg.

POTATO AND FENNEL SOUP WITH WARM ROSEMARY SCONES

THE SIMPLE FLAVOURS IN THIS FINE SOUP ARE ENHANCED BY THE DELICATE PERFUME OF HERB FLOWERS, AND COMPLEMENTED BY ROSEMARY-SEASONED SCONES.

SERVES 4

INGREDIENTS
75g/3oz/6 tbsp butter
2 onions, chopped
5ml/1 tsp fennel seeds, crushed
3 fennel bulbs, coarsely chopped
900g/2lb potatoes, thinly sliced
1.2 litres/2 pints/5 cups
  vegetable stock
150ml/¼ pint/⅔ cup double
  (heavy) cream
salt and ground black pepper
fresh herb flowers and 15ml/
  1 tbsp chopped fresh chives,
  to garnish

For the rosemary scones (biscuits)
225g/8oz/2 cups self-raising
  (self-rising) flour
2.5ml/½ tsp salt
5ml/1 tsp baking powder
10ml/2 tsp chopped fresh
  rosemary
50g/2oz/¼ cup butter
150ml/¼ pint/⅔ cup milk
1 egg, beaten, to glaze

1 Melt the butter in a pan. Add the onions and cook gently for 10 minutes, stirring occasionally, until very soft. Add the fennel seeds and cook for 2–3 minutes. Stir in the fennel and potatoes.

2 Cover the vegetables with a sheet of wet baking parchment and put a lid on the pan. Cook gently for 10 minutes until very soft.

3 Remove the parchment. Pour in the stock, bring to the boil, cover and simmer for 35 minutes.

4 Meanwhile, make the scones. Preheat the oven to 230°C/450°F/Gas 8 and grease a baking tray. Sift the flour, salt and baking powder into a bowl. Stir in the rosemary, then rub in the butter. Add the milk and mix to form a soft dough.

5 Knead very lightly on a floured surface. Roll out to 2cm/¾in thick. Stamp out 12 rounds with a cutter.

6 Brush with the egg and bake on the prepared baking tray for 8–10 minutes, until risen and golden. Cool on a wire rack until warm.

7 Leave the soup to cool slightly, then purée it in a food processor or blender until smooth. Press through a sieve (strainer) into the rinsed pan.

8 Stir in the cream with seasoning to taste. Reheat gently but do not boil.

9 Ladle the soup into four warmed soup bowls and scatter a few herb flowers and chopped chives over each. Serve immediately with the warm rosemary scones.

Energy 797Kcal/3332kJ; Protein 12.3g; Carbohydrate 84.1g, of which sugars 8.8g; Fat 48.1g, of which saturates 29.6g; Cholesterol 120mg; Calcium 316mg; Fibre 7.6g; Sodium 703mg.

PUMPKIN SOUP WITH RICE

PUMPKIN IS SO FULL OF COLOUR AND FLAVOUR THAT IT INSPIRES YOU TO BUY IT, GO HOME AND START COOKING THIS DELICIOUS WINTER SOUP.

SERVES 4

INGREDIENTS
 1.1kg/2lb 7oz pumpkin
 750ml/1¼ pints/3 cups
  chicken stock
 750ml/1¼ pints/3 cups semi-
  skimmed (low-fat) milk
 10–15ml/2–3 tsp sugar
 75g/3oz/½ cup cooked white rice
 salt and ground black pepper
 5ml/1 tsp ground cinnamon,
  to serve

1 Remove the seeds from the pumpkin, cut off the peel and chop the flesh.

2 Place in a pan and add the stock, milk, sugar and seasoning. Bring to the boil, then reduce the heat and simmer for about 20 minutes, or until the pumpkin is tender. Drain the pumpkin, reserving the liquid, and purée it in a food processor, then return it to the pan with the liquid.

3 Bring the soup back to the boil, throw in the rice and simmer for a few minutes. Check the seasoning, pour into bowls and dust with cinnamon.

Energy 202Kcal/856kJ; Protein 9.7g; Carbohydrate 33.1g, of which sugars 15.6g; Fat 4.4g, of which saturates 2.5g; Cholesterol 11mg; Calcium 315mg; Fibre 2.8g; Sodium 82mg.

CREAM OF CAULIFLOWER SOUP

THIS SOUP IS LIGHT IN FLAVOUR YET SATISFYING ENOUGH FOR A LUNCHTIME SNACK. YOU CAN TRY GREEN CAULIFLOWER FOR A COLOURFUL CHANGE.

SERVES 6

INGREDIENTS
30ml/2 tbsp olive oil
2 large onions, finely diced
1 garlic clove, crushed
3 large floury potatoes, finely diced
3 celery sticks, finely diced
1.75 litres/3 pints/7½ cups stock
2 carrots, finely diced
1 medium cauliflower, chopped
15ml/1 tbsp chopped fresh dill
15ml/1 tbsp lemon juice
5ml/1 tsp mustard powder
1.5ml/¼ tsp caraway seeds
300ml/½ pint/1¼ cups single
 (light) cream
salt and ground black pepper
shredded spring onions (scallions)

3 Add the cauliflower, fresh dill, lemon juice, mustard powder and caraway seeds to the pan and simmer gently for 20 minutes, until the vegetables are just tender.

4 Process the soup in a blender or food processor until smooth, return to the pan and stir in the cream. Season to taste and serve garnished with shredded spring onions.

1 Heat the oil in a large pan, add the onions and garlic and fry them for a few minutes until they soften. Add the potatoes, celery and stock and simmer for 10 minutes.

2 Add the carrots and simmer for a further 10 minutes.

Energy 258Kcal/1075kJ; Protein 6.9g; Carbohydrate 26.9g, of which sugars 9.8g; Fat 14.4g, of which saturates 6.9g; Cholesterol 28mg; Calcium 95mg; Fibre 3.8g; Sodium 46mg.

CURRIED CAULIFLOWER SOUP

THIS SPICY, CREAMY SOUP IS PERFECT FOR LUNCH ON A COLD WINTER'S DAY SERVED WITH CRUSTY BREAD AND GARNISHED WITH FRESH CORIANDER.

SERVES 4

INGREDIENTS
750ml/1¼ pints/3 cups milk
1 large cauliflower
15ml/1 tbsp garam masala
salt and ground black pepper

1 Pour the milk into a large pan and place over a medium heat. Cut the cauliflower into florets and add to the milk with the garam masala and season with salt and pepper.

2 Bring the milk to the boil, then reduce the heat, partially cover the pan with a lid and simmer for about 20 minutes, or until the cauliflower is tender.

3 Let the mixture cool for a few minutes, then transfer to a food processor and process until smooth (you may have to do this in two separate batches).

4 Return the purée to the pan and heat through gently without boiling, checking and adjusting the seasoning to taste. Serve immediately.

Energy 143Kcal/601kJ; Protein 12g; Carbohydrate 13.9g, of which sugars 12.6g; Fat 4.8g, of which saturates 2.3g; Cholesterol 11mg; Calcium 271mg; Fibre 3.2g; Sodium 104mg.

ROASTED GARLIC AND BUTTERNUT SQUASH SOUP WITH TOMATO SALSA

THIS IS A WONDERFUL, RICHLY FLAVOURED DISH. A SPOONFUL OF THE HOT AND SPICY TOMATO SALSA GIVES BITE TO THE SWEET-TASTING SQUASH AND GARLIC SOUP.

SERVES 4–5

INGREDIENTS
    2 garlic bulbs, outer skin removed
    75ml/5 tbsp olive oil
    a few fresh thyme sprigs
    1 large butternut squash, halved
        and seeded
    2 onions, chopped
    5ml/1 tsp ground coriander
    1.2 litres/2 pints/5 cups vegetable
        stock
    30–45ml/2–3 tbsp chopped fresh
        oregano or marjoram
    salt and ground black pepper
For the salsa
    4 large ripe tomatoes, halved
        and seeded
    1 red (bell) pepper, halved
        and seeded
    1 large fresh red chilli, halved
        and seeded
    30–45ml/2–3 tbsp extra virgin
        olive oil
    15ml/1 tbsp balsamic vinegar
    pinch of caster (superfine) sugar

1 Preheat the oven to 220°C/425°F/ Gas 7. Place the garlic bulbs on a piece of foil and pour over half the olive oil. Add the thyme sprigs, then fold the foil around the garlic bulbs to enclose them completely. Place the foil parcel on a baking sheet with the butternut squash and brush the squash with 15ml/1 tbsp of the remaining olive oil. Add the tomatoes, red pepper and fresh chilli for the salsa.

2 Roast the vegetables for 25 minutes, then remove the tomatoes, pepper and chilli. Reduce the temperature to 190°C/375°F/Gas 5 and cook the squash and garlic for 20–25 minutes more, or until the squash is tender.

3 Heat the remaining oil in a large, heavy-based pan and cook the onions and ground coriander gently for about 10 minutes, or until softened.

4 Skin the pepper and chilli and process in a food processor or blender with the tomatoes and 30ml/2 tbsp olive oil. Stir in the vinegar and seasoning to taste, adding a pinch of caster sugar. Add the remaining oil if you think the salsa needs it.

5 Squeeze the roasted garlic out of its papery skin into the onions and scoop the squash out of its skin, adding it to the pan. Add the stock, 5ml/1 tsp salt and plenty of black pepper. Bring to the boil and simmer for 10 minutes.

6 Stir in half the oregano or marjoram and cool the soup slightly, then process it in a blender or food processor. Alternatively, press the soup through a fine sieve (strainer).

7 Reheat the soup without allowing it to boil, then taste for seasoning before ladling it into warmed bowls. Top each with a spoonful of salsa and sprinkle over the remaining chopped oregano or marjoram. Serve immediately.

Energy 303Kcal/1256kJ; Protein 4.2g; Carbohydrate 20.7g, of which sugars 16.6g; Fat 23.2g, of which saturates 3.5g; Cholesterol 0mg; Calcium 107mg; Fibre 5.7g; Sodium 15mg.

SPICY ROASTED PUMPKIN SOUP
WITH PUMPKIN CRISPS

THE PUMPKIN IS ROASTED WHOLE, THEN SPLIT OPEN AND SCOOPED OUT TO MAKE THIS DELICIOUS SOUP; TOPPED WITH CRISP STRIPS OF FRIED PUMPKIN, IT IS A REAL TREAT.

SERVES 6–8

INGREDIENTS
    1.5kg/3–3½lb pumpkin
    90ml/6 tbsp olive oil
    2 onions, chopped
    3 garlic cloves, chopped
    7.5cm/3in piece fresh root
      ginger, grated
    5ml/1 tsp ground coriander
    2.5ml/½ tsp ground turmeric
    pinch of cayenne pepper
    1 litre/1¾ pints/4 cups
      vegetable stock
    salt and ground black pepper
    15ml/1 tbsp sesame seeds and
      fresh coriander (cilantro) leaves,
      to garnish
For the pumpkin crisps
    wedge of fresh pumpkin, seeded
    120ml/4fl oz/½ cup olive oil

1 Preheat the oven to 200°C/400°F/ Gas 6. Prick the pumpkin around the top several times with a fork. Brush the pumpkin with plenty of the oil and bake for 45 minutes or until tender. Leave until cool enough to handle.

2 Take care when cutting the pumpkin as there may still be a lot of hot steam inside. When cool enough to handle, scoop out and discard the seeds. Scoop out and chop the flesh.

3 Heat 60ml/4 tbsp of the remaining oil (you may not have to use all of it) in a large pan and add the onions, garlic and ginger, then cook gently for 4–5 minutes. Add the coriander, turmeric and cayenne, and cook for 2 minutes. Stir in the pumpkin flesh and stock. Bring to the boil, reduce the heat and simmer for 20 minutes.

COOK'S TIP
If only large pumpkins are available, cut off two or three large wedges weighing 1.5kg/3–3½lb in total. Brush with oil and roast for 20–30 minutes until tender.

4 Cool the soup slightly, then purée it in a food processor or blender until smooth. Return the soup to the rinsed pan and season well.

5 Meanwhile, prepare the pumpkin crisps. Using a swivel-blade potato peeler, pare off long thin strips.

6 Heat the oil in a small pan and fry the strips in batches for 2–3 minutes, until crisp. Drain on kitchen paper.

7 Reheat the soup and ladle it into bowls. Top with the pumpkin crisps and garnish each portion with sesame seeds and coriander leaves.

Energy 271Kcal/1119kJ; Protein 3.1g; Carbohydrate 11.1g, of which sugars 8.2g; Fat 24.1g, of which saturates 3.6g; Cholesterol 0mg; Calcium 110mg; Fibre 3.8g; Sodium 3mg.

FRESH TOMATO SOUP

THE COMBINATION OF INTENSELY FLAVOURED SUN-RIPENED AND FRESH TOMATOES NEEDS LITTLE
EMBELLISHMENT IN THIS TASTY ITALIAN SOUP. CHOOSE THE RIPEST-LOOKING TOMATOES.

SERVES 6

INGREDIENTS

1.3–1.6kg/3–3½lb ripe tomatoes
400ml/14fl oz/1⅔ cups vegetable
  stock
45ml/3 tbsp sun-dried tomato
  purée (paste)
30–45ml/2–3 tbsp balsamic vinegar
10–15ml/2–3 tsp sugar
a small handful of fresh basil leaves,
  plus extra to garnish
salt and ground black pepper
toasted cheese croûtes and crème
  fraîche, to serve

COOK'S TIP
Use a sharp knife to cut a cross in the
base of each tomato before plunging it
into the boiling water. The skin will then
peel back easily from the crosses.

1 Plunge the tomatoes into boiling
water for 30 seconds, then refresh
in cold water. Peel off the skins and
quarter the tomatoes. Put them in a
large pan and pour over the chicken or
vegetable stock. Bring just to the boil,
reduce the heat, cover and simmer
gently for 10 minutes until the tomatoes
are pulpy.

2 Stir in the tomato purée, vinegar,
sugar and basil. Season with salt
and pepper, then cook gently, stirring,
for 2 minutes. Process the soup in a
blender or food processor, then return
to a clean pan and reheat gently. Serve
in bowls, topped with one or two toasted
cheese croûtes and a spoonful of crème
fraîche, garnished with basil leaves.

Energy 52Kcal/225kJ; Protein 1.9g; Carbohydrate 10.4g, of which sugars 10.4g; Fat 0.7g, of which saturates 0.2g; Cholesterol 0mg; Calcium 19mg; Fibre 2.4g; Sodium 38mg.

TOMATO SOUP WITH RED PEPPER CREAM

THIS DAZZLING SOUP CAN BE MADE AS FIERY OR AS MILD AS YOU LIKE BY INCREASING OR REDUCING THE NUMBER OF CHILLIES.

4 Transfer the pepper for the pepper cream to a bowl as soon as it is cooked. Cover with clear film (plastic wrap) and leave to cool. Peel away the skin and purée the flesh in a food processor or blender with half the crème fraîche. Pour into a bowl and stir in the remaining crème fraîche. Season and add a dash of Tabasco sauce. Chill in the refrigerator until required.

5 Process the roasted vegetables in batches, adding a ladleful of stock to each batch to make a smooth, thick purée. Depending on how juicy the tomatoes are, you may not need all the vegetable stock.

6 Press the purée through a sieve (strainer) into a pan and stir in more stock if you want to thin the soup. Heat gently and season well. Ladle the soup into bowls and spoon red pepper cream into the centre of each bowl. Pile wild rocket leaves on top to garnish.

SERVES 4

INGREDIENTS
1.5kg/3–3½lb plum tomatoes, halved
5 red chillies, seeded
1 red (bell) pepper, halved
  and seeded
2 red onions, roughly chopped
6 garlic cloves, crushed
30ml/2 tbsp sun-dried tomato paste
45ml/3 tbsp olive oil
400ml/14fl oz/1⅔ cups
  vegetable stock
salt and ground black pepper
wild rocket (arugula), to garnish
For the pepper cream
  1 red pepper, halved and
    seeded
  10ml/2 tsp olive oil
  120ml/4fl oz/½ cup crème fraîche
  a few drops of Tabasco sauce

1 Preheat the oven to 200°C/400°F/ Gas 6. Place the tomatoes, chillies, red pepper, onions, garlic and tomato paste in a roasting tin (pan). Toss all the vegetables, drizzle with the oil and toss again, then roast for 40 minutes, until tender and the pepper skin is slightly charred.

2 Meanwhile make the pepper cream. Lay the red pepper halves skin side up on a baking tray and brush with the olive oil.

3 Roast with the mixed vegetables for about 30–40 minutes, until blistered.

COOK'S TIP
The pepper cream may be a bit runny when first processed, but it firms up when chilled.

Energy 319Kcal/1330kJ; Protein 5.3g; Carbohydrate 23.5g, of which sugars 22g; Fat 23.4g, of which saturates 10g; Cholesterol 34mg; Calcium 67mg; Fibre 6.2g; Sodium 72mg.

TOMATO SOUP WITH BLACK OLIVE CIABATTA TOASTS

TOMATO SOUP IS EVERYBODY'S FAVOURITE, PARTICULARLY WHEN MADE WITH FRESH SUN-RIPENED TOMATOES. THIS DELICIOUS SOUP IS WONDERFULLY WARMING AND HAS AN EARTHY RICHNESS.

SERVES 6

INGREDIENTS
   450g/1lb very ripe fresh tomatoes
   30ml/2 tbsp olive oil
   1 onion, chopped
   1 garlic clove, crushed
   30ml/2 tbsp sherry vinegar
   30ml/2 tbsp tomato purée (paste)
   15ml/1 tbsp cornflour (cornstarch)
      or potato flour
   300ml/½ pint/1¼ cups passata
      (bottled strained tomatoes)
   1 bay leaf
   900ml/1½ pints/3¾ cups vegetable
      stock
   200ml/7fl oz/scant 1 cup crème fraîche
   salt and ground black pepper
   basil leaves, to garnish
For the black olive ciabatta toasts
   1 plain or black olive ciabatta
   1 small red (bell) pepper
   3 whole garlic cloves, skins on
   225g/8oz black olives (preferably
      a wrinkly Greek variety)
   30–45ml/2–3 tbsp salted capers or
      capers in vinegar
   12 drained canned anchovy fillets
      or 1 small can tuna in oil, drained
   about 150ml/¼ pint/⅔ cup good-
      quality olive oil
   fresh lemon juice and ground black
      pepper, to taste
   45ml/3 tbsp chopped fresh basil

1 Make the ciabatta toasts first. Preheat the oven to 200°C/400°F/Gas 6. Split the ciabatta in half and cut each half into nine fingers to give 18 in total. Arrange on a baking sheet and bake for 10–15 minutes until golden and crisp.

2 Place the whole pepper and garlic cloves under a hot grill (broiler) and cook for 15 minutes, turning, until charred all over. If you prefer, you can bake them in the oven for about 25 minutes. Once charred, put the garlic and pepper in a plastic bag, seal and leave to cool for about 10 minutes.

3 When the pepper is cool, peel off the skin (do not wash) and remove the stalk and seeds. Peel the skin off the garlic. Stone (pit) the olives. Rinse the capers under running water to remove the salt or vinegar. Place the prepared ingredients in a food processor with the anchovies or tuna and process until roughly chopped.

4 With the machine running, slowly add the olive oil until you have a fairly smooth dark paste. Alternatively, just stir in the olive oil for a chunkier result. Season to taste with lemon juice and pepper. Stir in the basil.

5 Spread the paste on the finger toasts, or, if not using immediately, transfer to a jar, cover with a layer of olive oil and keep in the refrigerator for up to three weeks.

6 For the soup, cut the tomatoes in half and remove the seeds and pulp using a lemon squeezer. Press the pulp through a sieve (strainer) and reserve the liquid.

7 Heat the oil in a pan and add the onion, garlic, sherry vinegar, tomato purée and the tomato halves. Stir, then cover the pan and cook over a low heat for 1 hour, stirring occasionally. When done, process the soup in a blender or food processor until smooth, then pass through a sieve to remove any pieces of skin. Return to the pan.

8 Mix the cornflour or potato flour with the reserved tomato pulp, then stir into the hot soup with the passata, bay leaf and stock. Simmer for 30 minutes. Stir in the crème fraîche and garnish with the basil leaves. Serve piping hot, with the ciabatta toasts.

Energy 532Kcal/2211kJ; Protein 11.9g; Carbohydrate 29.3g, of which sugars 7.6g; Fat 41.7g, of which saturates 13.2g; Cholesterol 50mg; Calcium 120mg; Fibre 3.5g; Sodium 1352mg.

BABY CHERRY TOMATO SOUP
<u>WITH</u> ROCKET PESTO

FOR THEIR SIZE, BABY TOMATOES ARE A POWERHOUSE OF SWEETNESS AND FLAVOUR. HERE THEY ARE COMPLEMENTED BEAUTIFULLY BY A RICH PASTE OF PEPPERY ROCKET.

SERVES 4

INGREDIENTS
   225g/8oz baby cherry
      tomatoes, halved
   225g/8oz baby plum tomatoes, halved
   225g/8oz vine-ripened
      tomatoes, halved
   2 shallots, roughly chopped
   25ml/1½ tbsp sun-dried
      tomato paste
   600ml/1 pint/2½ cups
      vegetable stock
   salt and ground black pepper
   ice cubes, to serve
For the pesto
   15g/½oz rocket (arugula) leaves
   75ml/5 tbsp olive oil
   15g/½oz/2 tbsp pine nuts
   1 garlic clove
   25g/1oz/⅓ cup freshly grated
      Parmesan cheese

1 Purée all the tomatoes and the shallots in a food processor or blender. Add the sun-dried tomato paste and process until smooth. Press the purée through a sieve (strainer) into a pan.

2 Add the vegetable stock, bring to the boil and simmer gently for 4–5 minutes. Season well with salt and black pepper. Leave to cool, then chill in the refrigerator for at least 4 hours.

3 To make the pesto, purée the rocket, oil, pine nuts and garlic using a mortar and pestle. Alternatively, use a food processor.

4 Stir the Parmesan cheese into the pesto mix, grinding it well.

5 Ladle the soup into bowls and add a few ice cubes to each. Spoon some of the rocket pesto into the centre of each portion and serve.

VARIATION
The pesto can be made with other soft-leaved herbs in place of rocket. Try fresh basil, coriander (cilantro) or mint, or use a mixture of herb leaves, if you like. Parsley and mint are a good flavour combination and make delicious pesto.

Energy 197Kcal/819kJ; Protein 4.9g; Carbohydrate 7.9g, of which sugars 7.6g; Fat 16.5g, of which saturates 3.3g; Cholesterol 6mg; Calcium 101mg; Fibre 2.4g; Sodium 105mg.

TOMATO, CIABATTA AND BASIL OIL SOUP

THROUGHOUT EUROPE, BREAD IS A POPULAR INGREDIENT FOR THICKENING SOUP, AND THIS RECIPE SHOWS HOW WONDERFULLY QUICK AND EASY THIS METHOD CAN BE.

SERVES 4

INGREDIENTS
    45ml/3 tbsp olive oil
    1 red onion, chopped
    6 garlic cloves, chopped
    300ml/½ pint/1¼ cups white wine
    150ml/¼ pint/⅔ cup water
    12 plum tomatoes, quartered
    2 x 400g/14oz cans plum tomatoes
    2.5ml/½ tsp sugar
    ½ ciabatta loaf
    salt and ground black pepper
    basil leaves, to garnish
For the basil oil
    115g/4oz basil leaves
    120ml/4fl oz/½ cup olive oil

1 For the basil oil, process the basil and oil in a food processor or blender to make a paste. Line a bowl with muslin (cheesecloth) and scrape the paste into it. Gather up the muslin and squeeze firmly to extract all the oil. Set aside.

2 Heat the oil in a large pan and cook the onion and garlic for 4–5 minutes until softened.

3 Add the wine, water, fresh and canned tomatoes. Bring to the boil, reduce the heat and cover the pan, then simmer for 3–4 minutes. Add the sugar and season well with salt and black pepper.

4 Break the bread into bite-sized pieces and stir into the soup.

5 Ladle the soup into bowls. Garnish with basil and drizzle the basil oil over each portion.

Energy 332Kcal/1396kJ; Protein 7.8g; Carbohydrate 35.4g, of which sugars 16.3g; Fat 13.4g, of which saturates 2g; Cholesterol 0mg; Calcium 98mg; Fibre 5g; Sodium 306mg.

ROASTED PEPPER SOUP
WITH PARMESAN TOAST

THE SECRET OF THIS SOUP IS TO SERVE IT JUST COLD, NOT OVER-CHILLED, TOPPED WITH HOT PARMESAN TOAST DRIPPING WITH CHEESE AND MELTED BUTTER.

SERVES 4

INGREDIENTS
  1 onion, quartered
  4 garlic cloves, unpeeled
  2 red (bell) peppers, seeded
    and quartered
  2 yellow (bell) peppers, seeded
    and quartered
  30–45ml/2–3 tbsp olive oil
  grated rind and juice of 1 orange
  200g/7oz can chopped tomatoes
  600ml/1 pint/2½ cups cold water
  salt and ground black pepper
  30ml/2 tbsp chopped fresh chives,
    to garnish (optional)
For the hot Parmesan toast
  1 medium baguette
  50g/2oz/¼ cup butter
  175g/6oz Parmesan cheese

1 Preheat the oven to 200°C/400°F/ Gas 6. Put the onion, garlic and peppers in a roasting tin (pan). Drizzle the oil over the vegetables and mix well, then turn the pieces of pepper skin sides up. Roast for 25–30 minutes, until slightly charred, then allow to cool slightly.

2 Squeeze the garlic flesh out of the skins into a food processor or blender. Add the roasted vegetables, orange rind and juice, tomatoes and water. Process until smooth.

COOK'S TIP
If you don't have a champignon, then use the bottom of a large ladle or the back of a wooden spoon instead.

3 Press the mixture through a sieve into a bowl using a champignon. Season well and chill for 30 minutes.

4 Make the Parmesan toasts when you are ready to serve the soup. Preheat the grill (broiler) to high. Tear the baguette in half lengthways, then tear or cut it across to give four large pieces. Spread the pieces of bread with butter.

5 Pare most of the Parmesan into thin slices or shavings using a swivel-bladed vegetable knife or a small paring knife, then finely grate the remainder.

6 Arrange the sliced Parmesan on the toasts, then dredge with the grated cheese.Transfer the cheese-topped baguette pieces to a large baking sheet or grill (broiler) rack and toast under the grill for a few minutes until the topping is well browned.

7 Ladle the chilled soup into large, shallow bowls and sprinkle with chopped fresh chives, if using, and plenty of freshly ground black pepper.

8 Serve the craggy hot Parmesan toast with the chilled soup.

Energy 124Kcal/516kJ; Protein 2.4g; Carbohydrate 15g, of which sugars 14.2g; Fat 6.4g, of which saturates 1g; Cholesterol 0mg; Calcium 23mg; Fibre 3.5g; Sodium 13mg.

SUMMER HERB SOUP <u>WITH</u> CHARGRILLED RADICCHIO

THE SWEETNESS OF SHALLOTS AND LEEKS IN THIS SOUP IS BALANCED BEAUTIFULLY BY THE SLIGHTLY ACIDIC SORREL WITH ITS HINT OF LEMON, AND A BOUQUET OF SUMMER HERBS.

SERVES 4–6

INGREDIENTS
  30ml/2 tbsp dry white wine
  2 shallots, finely chopped
  1 garlic clove, crushed
  2 leeks, sliced
  1 large potato, about 225g/8oz,
    roughly chopped
  2 courgettes (zucchini), chopped
  600ml/1 pint/2½ cups water
  115g/4oz sorrel, torn
  large handful of fresh chervil
  large handful of fresh flat leaf parsley
  large handful of fresh mint
  1 round (butterhead) lettuce,
    separated into leaves
  600ml/1 pint/2½ cups
    vegetable stock
  1 small head of radicchio
  5ml/1 tsp groundnut (peanut) oil
  salt and ground black pepper

1 Put the wine, shallots and garlic into a heavy-based pan and bring to the boil. Cook for 2–3 minutes, until softened.

2 Add the leeks, potato and courgette with enough of the water to come about halfway up the vegetables. Lay a wetted piece of greaseproof paper over the vegetables and put a lid on the pan, then cook for 10–15 minutes, until soft.

3 Remove the paper and add the fresh herbs and lettuce. Cook for 1–2 minutes, or until wilted.

4 Pour in the remaining water and the vegetable stock and simmer for 10–12 minutes. Cool the soup slightly, then process it in a food processor or blender until smooth. Return the soup to the rinsed-out pan and season well.

5 Cut the radicchio into thin wedges that hold together, then brush the cut sides with the oil. Heat a ridged griddle or frying pan until very hot and add the radicchio wedges.

6 Cook the radicchio for 1 minute on each side until slightly charred. Reheat the soup over a low heat, then ladle it into warmed shallow bowls. Serve a wedge of charred radicchio on top.

Energy 102Kcal/428kJ; Protein 5g; Carbohydrate 15.1g, of which sugars 5.7g; Fat 2.2g, of which saturates 0.4g; Cholesterol 0mg; Calcium 135mg; Fibre 4.9g; Sodium 57mg.

AUBERGINE SOUP WITH MOZZARELLA AND GREMOLATA

GREMOLATA, A CLASSIC ITALIAN MIXTURE OF GARLIC, LEMON AND PARSLEY, ADDS A FLOURISH OF FRESH FLAVOUR TO THIS RICH CREAM SOUP.

SERVES 6

INGREDIENTS
    30ml/2 tbsp olive oil
    2 shallots, chopped
    2 garlic cloves, chopped
    1kg/2¼lb aubergines (eggplant),
       trimmed and roughly chopped
    1 litre/1¾ pints/4 cups
       vegetable stock
    150ml/¼ pint/⅔ cup double
       (heavy) cream
    30ml/2 tbsp chopped
       fresh parsley
    175g/6oz buffalo mozzarella,
       thinly sliced
    salt and ground black pepper

For the gremolata
    2 garlic cloves, finely chopped
    grated rind of 2 lemons
    15ml/1 tbsp chopped fresh parsley

1 Heat the oil in a large pan and add the shallots and garlic. Cook for 4–5 minutes, until soft. Add the aubergines and cook for about 25 minutes, stirring occasionally, until soft and browned.

2 Pour in the stock and cook for about 5 minutes. Leave the soup to cool slightly, then purée in a food processor or blender until smooth. Return to the rinsed pan and season. Add the cream and parsley and bring to the boil.

3 Mix the ingredients for the gremolata in a small bowl.

4 Ladle the soup into bowls and lay the mozzarella on top. Scatter with gremolata and serve.

Energy 261Kcal/1079kJ; Protein 7.5g; Carbohydrate 4.9g, of which sugars 4.3g; Fat 23.7g, of which saturates 13.1g; Cholesterol 51mg; Calcium 137mg; Fibre 3.5g; Sodium 124mg.

SIMPLE CREAM OF ONION SOUP

THIS WONDERFULLY SOOTHING SOUP HAS A DEEP, BUTTERY FLAVOUR THAT IS COMPLEMENTED BY CRISP CROÛTONS OR CHOPPED CHIVES, SPRINKLED OVER JUST BEFORE SERVING.

SERVES 4

INGREDIENTS

115g/4oz/½ cup unsalted butter
1kg/2¼lb yellow onions, sliced
1 fresh bay leaf
105ml/7 tbsp dry white vermouth
1 litre/1¾ pints/4 cups good
  vegetable stock
150ml/¼ pint/⅔ cup double
  (heavy) cream
a little lemon juice (optional)
salt and ground black pepper
croûtons or chopped fresh chives,
  to garnish

COOK'S TIP
Adding the second batch of onions gives texture and a buttery flavour to this soup. Make sure they do not brown.

1 Melt 75g/3oz/6 tbsp of the butter in a large heavy-based pan. Set about 200g/7oz of the onions aside and add the rest to the pan with the bay leaf. Stir to coat in the butter, then cover and cook very gently for about 30 minutes. The onions should be very soft and tender, but not browned.

2 Add the vermouth, increase the heat and boil rapidly until the liquid has evaporated. Add the stock, 5ml/1 tsp salt and pepper to taste. Bring to the boil, lower the heat and simmer for 5 minutes, then remove from the heat.

3 Leave to cool, then discard the bay leaf and process the soup in a blender or food processor. Return the soup to the rinsed pan.

4 Meanwhile, melt the remaining butter in another pan and cook the remaining onions slowly, covered, until soft but not browned. Uncover and continue to cook gently until golden yellow.

5 Add the cream to the soup and reheat it gently until hot, but do not allow it to boil. Taste and adjust the seasoning, adding a little lemon juice if liked. Add the buttery onions and stir for 1–2 minutes, then ladle the soup into bowls. Sprinkle with croûtons or chopped chives and serve.

Energy 519Kcal/2139kJ; Protein 3.8g; Carbohydrate 21.4g, of which sugars 15.6g; Fat 44.3g, of which saturates 27.5g; Cholesterol 113mg; Calcium 88mg; Fibre 3.5g; Sodium 193mg.

SHERRIED ONION AND ALMOND SOUP WITH SAFFRON

*THE SPANISH COMBINATION OF ONIONS, SHERRY AND SAFFRON GIVES THIS PALE YELLOW SOUP
A BEGUILING FLAVOUR THAT IS PERFECT AS THE OPENING COURSE OF A SPECIAL MEAL.*

2 Add the saffron strands and cook, uncovered, for 3–4 minutes, then add the ground almonds and cook, stirring constantly, for another 2–3 minutes. Pour in the stock and sherry and stir in 5ml/1 tsp salt. Season with plenty of black pepper. Bring to the boil, then lower the heat and simmer gently for about 10 minutes.

SERVES 4

INGREDIENTS
40g/1½oz/3 tbsp butter
2 large yellow onions, thinly sliced
1 small garlic clove, finely chopped
good pinch of saffron strands (about 12 strands)
50g/2oz blanched almonds, toasted and finely ground
750ml/1¼ pints/3 cups good vegetable stock
45ml/3 tbsp dry sherry
salt and ground black pepper
30ml/2 tbsp flaked or slivered almonds, toasted and chopped, and fresh parsley, to garnish

1 Melt the butter in a heavy-based pan over a low heat. Add the onions and garlic, stirring to coat them thoroughly in the butter, then cover the pan and cook very gently, stirring frequently, for 15–20 minutes, until the onions are a soft texture and golden yellow in colour.

VARIATION
This soup is also delicious served chilled. Use olive oil rather than butter and add a little more chicken or vegetable stock to make a slightly thinner soup, then leave to cool and chill for at least 4 hours. Just before serving, taste for seasoning. Float 1–2 ice cubes in each bowl.

3 Process the soup in a blender or food processor until smooth, then return it to the rinsed pan. Reheat slowly, stirring occasionally, but do not allow the soup to boil. Taste for seasoning, adding more salt and pepper if required.

4 Ladle the soup into heated bowls, garnish with the toasted flaked or slivered almonds and a little parsley, and serve immediately.

Energy 255Kcal/1054kJ; Protein 5.8g; Carbohydrate 11.5g, of which sugars 8.1g; Fat 19.6g, of which saturates 6.1g; Cholesterol 21mg; Calcium 82mg; Fibre 3.2g; Sodium 68mg.

POTATO AND ROASTED GARLIC BROTH

ROASTED GARLIC TAKES ON A SUBTLE, SWEET FLAVOUR IN THIS DELICIOUS VEGETARIAN SOUP. SERVE IT PIPING HOT WITH MELTED CHEDDAR OR GRUYÈRE CHEESE ON FRENCH BREAD, AS A WINTER WARMER.

SERVES 4

INGREDIENTS

   2 small or 1 large whole head of
     garlic (about 20 cloves)
   4 medium potatoes (about 500g/
     1¼lb in total), diced
   1.75 litres/3 pints/7½ cups
     good-quality hot vegetable stock
   chopped flat leaf parsley, to garnish

COOK'S TIP
Choose floury potatoes such as Maris Piper, Estima, Cara or King Edward to give the soup a delicious velvety texture.

VARIATION
If you are not a vegetarian, you can use chicken or beef stock for a slightly different flavour.

1 Preheat the oven to 190°C/375°F/ Gas 5. Place the unpeeled garlic bulbs or bulb in a small roasting tin (pan) and bake for 30 minutes until soft in the centre.

2 Meanwhile, par-boil the potatoes in a large pan of lightly salted boiling water for 10 minutes.

3 Simmer the stock in another pan for 5 minutes. Drain the potatoes and add them to the stock.

4 Squeeze the garlic pulp into the soup, reserving a few whole cloves, stir and season to taste. Simmer for 15 minutes and serve topped with the whole garlic cloves and parsley.

Energy 115Kcal/488kJ; Protein 4.3g; Carbohydrate 24.3g, of which sugars 2.1g; Fat 0.7g, of which saturates 0.2g; Cholesterol 0mg; Calcium 14mg; Fibre 2.3g; Sodium 219mg.

GARLIC SOUP WITH EGG AND CROÛTONS

SPANISH SOUP AND ITALIAN POLENTA MARRY WONDERFULLY WELL IN THIS RECIPE. THE DELICIOUS GARLIC SOUP ORIGINATES FROM ANDALUSIA IN SPAIN.

SERVES 4

INGREDIENTS
15ml/1 tbsp olive oil
1 garlic bulb, unpeeled and broken into cloves
4 slices day-old ciabatta bread, broken into pieces
1.2 litres/2 pints/5 cups vegetble stock
pinch of saffron
15ml/1 tbsp white wine vinegar
4 eggs
salt and ground black pepper
chopped fresh parsley, to garnish
For the polenta
750ml/1¼ pints/3 cups milk
175g/6oz/1 cup quick-cook polenta
50g/2oz/¼ cup butter

1 Preheat the oven to 200°C/400°F/ Gas 6. Brush the oil over a roasting tin (pan), then add the garlic and bread, and roast for about 20 minutes, until the garlic is soft and the bread is dry. Leave until cool enough to handle.

2 Meanwhile, make the polenta. Bring the milk to the boil in a large, heavy-based pan and gradually pour in the polenta, stirring constantly. Cook for about 5 minutes, or according to the packet instructions, stirring frequently, until the polenta begins to come away from the side of the pan.

3 Spoon the polenta on to a chopping board and spread out to about 1cm/½in thick. Allow to cool and set, then cut into 1cm/½in dice.

4 Squeeze the garlic cloves from their skins into a food processor or blender. Add the dried bread and 300ml/½ pint/1¼ cups of the stock, then process until smooth. Pour into a pan. Pound the saffron in a mortar and stir in a little of the remaining stock, then add to the soup with enough of the remaining stock to thin the soup as required.

5 Melt the butter in a frying pan and cook the diced polenta over a high heat for 1–2 minutes, tossing until beginning to brown. Drain on kitchen paper.

6 Season the soup and reheat gently. Bring a large frying pan of water to the boil. Add the vinegar and reduce the heat to a simmer. Crack an egg on to a saucer. Swirl the water with a knife and drop the egg into the middle of the swirl. Repeat with the remaining eggs and poach for 2–3 minutes until set. Lift out the eggs using a draining spoon, then place one in each of four bowls.

7 Ladle the soup over the poached eggs, scatter polenta croûtons and parsley on top and serve.

Energy 415Kcal/1731kJ; Protein 13.4g; Carbohydrate 43.9g, of which sugars 0.9g; Fat 20.8g, of which saturates 8.6g; Cholesterol 217mg; Calcium 57mg; Fibre 1.9g; Sodium 247mg.

CHUNKY VEGETABLE SOUPS

In this section you will find a collection of traditional
European soups such as Irish Leek and Blue Cheese Soup,
Portuguese Garlic Soup, and the classic Jewish Sweet and Sour
Cabbage, Beetroot and Tomato Borscht. You can also try the
more exotic vegetable soups of Goa and Thailand. Ingredients
such as mooli (daikon), wild mushrooms and Chinese leaves
(Chinese cabbage) are readily available in many supermarkets
these days, so be adventurous and try something new.

CORN AND POTATO CHOWDER

THIS CREAMY YET CHUNKY SOUP IS RICH WITH THE SWEET TASTE OF CORN. IT'S EXCELLENT SERVED WITH THICK CRUSTY BREAD AND TOPPED WITH SOME MELTED CHEDDAR CHEESE.

SERVES 4

INGREDIENTS

1 onion, chopped
1 garlic clove, crushed
1 medium baking potato, chopped
2 celery sticks, sliced
1 small green (bell) pepper, seeded,
 halved and sliced
30ml/2 tbsp sunflower oil
25g/1oz/2 tbsp butter
600ml/1 pint/2½ cups stock or water
300ml/½ pint/1¼ cups milk
200g/7oz can flageolet beans
300g/11oz can corn kernels
good pinch dried sage
salt and ground black pepper
Cheddar cheese, grated, to serve

1 Put the onion, garlic, potato, celery and green pepper into a large heavy-based pan with the oil and butter.

2 Heat the ingredients until sizzling then reduce the heat to low. Cover and cook gently for about 10 minutes, shaking the pan occasionally to prevent the ingredients sticking.

3 Pour in the stock or water, season with salt and pepper to taste and bring to the boil. Reduce the heat, cover again and simmer gently for about 15 minutes until the vegetables are tender.

4 Add the milk, beans and corn – including their liquids – and the sage. Simmer, uncovered, for 5 minutes. Check the seasoning and serve hot, sprinkled with grated cheese.

Energy 251Kcal/1052kJ; Protein 9.7g; Carbohydrate 25.9g, of which sugars 9.3g; Fat 12.9g, of which saturates 4.9g; Cholesterol 18mg; Calcium 128mg; Fibre 5.5g; Sodium 1154mg.

CORN AND RED CHILLI CHOWDER

CORN AND CHILLIES MAKE GOOD BEDFELLOWS, AND HERE THE COOL COMBINATION OF CREAMED CORN AND MILK IS THE PERFECT FOIL FOR THE RAGING HEAT OF THE CHILLIES.

SERVES 6

INGREDIENTS
    2 tomatoes, skinned
    1 onion, roughly chopped
    375g/13oz can creamed corn
    2 red (bell) peppers, halved
      and seeded
    15ml/1 tbsp olive oil, plus extra
      for brushing
    3 red chillies, seeded and sliced
    2 garlic cloves, chopped
    5ml/1 tsp ground cumin
    5ml/1 tsp ground coriander
    600ml/1 pint/2½ cups milk
    350ml/12fl oz/1½ cups
      vegetable stock
    3 cobs of corn, kernels removed
    450g/1lb potatoes, finely diced
    60ml/4 tbsp double (heavy) cream
    60ml/4 tbsp chopped fresh
      parsley
    salt and ground black pepper

1 Process the tomatoes and onion in a food processor or blender to a smooth purée. Add the creamed sweetcorn and process again, then set aside. Preheat the grill (broiler) to high.

2 Put the peppers, skin sides up, on a grill rack and brush with oil. Grill (broil) for 8–10 minutes, until the skins blacken and blister. Transfer to a bowl and cover with clear film (plastic wrap), then leave to cool. Peel and dice the peppers, then set them aside.

3 Heat the oil in a large pan and add the chillies and garlic. Cook, stirring, for 2–3 minutes, until softened.

4 Add the ground cumin and coriander, and cook for a further 1 minute. Stir in the sweetcorn purée and cook for about 8 minutes, stirring occasionally.

5 Pour in the milk and stock, then stir in the corn kernels, potatoes, red pepper and seasoning to taste. Cook for 15–20 minutes, until the corn and potatoes are tender.

6 Pour into deep bowls and add the cream, then sprinkle over the chopped parsley and serve at once.

Energy 343Kcal/1448kJ; Protein 9.4g; Carbohydrate 55.4g, of which sugars 23.2g; Fat 10.9g, of which saturates 5.1g; Cholesterol 20mg; Calcium 147mg; Fibre 4g; Sodium 383mg.

IRISH LEEK AND BLUE CHEESE SOUP

THE BLUE CHEESE IS AN INTEGRAL PART OF THIS SUBSTANTIAL SOUP, WHICH MAKES FULL USE OF INGREDIENTS THAT HAVE ALWAYS BEEN IMPORTANT IN IRISH COOKING. IT CAN BE A GOOD WAY TO USE UP CHEESES LEFT OVER FROM THE CHEESEBOARD. SERVE WITH FRESHLY BAKED BROWN BREAD.

SERVES 6

INGREDIENTS
    3 large leeks
    50g/2oz/¼ cup butter
    30ml/2 tbsp oil
    115g/4oz Irish blue cheese,
        such as Cashel Blue
    15g/½oz/2 tbsp plain
        (all-purpose) flour
    15ml/1 tbsp wholegrain Irish
        mustard, or to taste
    1.5 litres/2½ pints/6¼ cups
        vegetable stock
    ground black pepper
    50g/2oz/½ cup grated cheese and
        chopped chives or spring onion
        (scallion) greens, to garnish

VARIATION
Any melting blue-veined cheese can be used in this recipe, such as Cabrales, Gorgonzola or Picon.

1 Slice the leeks thinly. Heat the butter and oil together in a large heavy pan and gently cook the leeks in it, covered, for 10–15 minutes, or until just softened but not brown.

2 Grate the cheese coarsely and add it to the pan, stirring over a low heat until it is melted. Add the flour and cook for 2 minutes, stirring constantly with a wooden spoon, then add ground black pepper and mustard to taste.

3 Gradually add the stock, stirring constantly and blending it in well; bring the soup to the boil.

4 Reduce the heat, cover and simmer very gently for about 15 minutes. Check the seasoning.

5 Serve the soup garnished with the extra grated cheese and the chopped chives or spring onion greens, and hand fresh bread around separately.

Energy 205Kcal/852kJ; Protein 8.2g; Carbohydrate 7.9g, of which sugars 2.2g; Fat 15.7g, of which saturates 9.9g; Cholesterol 40mg; Calcium 188mg; Fibre 2.2g; Sodium 347mg.

LEEK AND OATMEAL SOUP

THIS TRADITIONAL IRISH SOUP IS KNOWN AS BROTCHÁN FOLTCHEP OR BROTCHÁN ROY, AND COMBINES LEEKS, OATMEAL AND MILK — THREE INGREDIENTS THAT HAVE BEEN STAPLE FOODS IN IRELAND FOR CENTURIES. SERVE WITH FRESHLY BAKED BREAD AND BUTTER.

SERVES 4–6

INGREDIENTS
   about 1.2 litres/2 pints/5 cups
      vegetable stock and milk, mixed
   30ml/2 tbsp medium pinhead
      oatmeal
   25g/1oz/2 tbsp butter
   6 large leeks, sliced into 2cm/¾ in
      pieces and washed
   sea salt and ground black pepper
   pinch of ground mace
   30ml/2 tbsp chopped fresh parsley
   single (light) cream and chopped
      fresh parsley leaves or chives,
      to garnish

1 Bring the stock and milk mixture to the boil over medium heat and sprinkle in the oatmeal. Stir well to prevent lumps forming, and then simmer gently.

2 Melt the butter in a separate pan and cook the leeks over a gentle heat until softened slightly, then add them to the stock. Simmer for 15–20 minutes, until the oatmeal is cooked.

VARIATION
Make nettle soup in the spring, when the nettle tops are young and tender. Strip about 10oz/275g nettle tops from the stems, chop them and add to the leeks.

3 Season with salt, pepper and mace, stir in the parsley and serve in warmed bowls. Decorate with a swirl of cream and some chopped fresh parsley or chives, if you like.

Energy 121Kcal/505kJ; Protein 4.2g; Carbohydrate 11.3g, of which sugars 4.5g; Fat 6.8g, of which saturates 3.5g; Cholesterol 13mg; Calcium 53mg; Fibre 4.9g; Sodium 44mg.

PORTUGUESE GARLIC SOUP

THIS RECIPE IS BASED ON THE WONDERFUL BREAD SOUPS OR AÇORDAS OF PORTUGAL. BEING A SIMPLE SOUP IT SHOULD BE MADE WITH THE BEST INGREDIENTS — PLUMP GARLIC, FRESH CORIANDER, HIGH-QUALITY CRUSTY COUNTRY BREAD AND EXTRA VIRGIN OLIVE OIL.

SERVES 6

INGREDIENTS

  25g/1oz fresh coriander (cilantro),
    leaves and stalks chopped separately
  1.5 litres/2½ pints/6¼ cups vegetable
    stock, or water
  5–6 plump garlic cloves, peeled
  6 eggs
  275g/10oz day-old bread, most
    of the crust removed, torn into
    bite-size pieces
  salt and ground black pepper
  90ml/6 tbsp extra virgin olive oil,
    plus extra to serve

1 Place the coriander stalks in a pan. Add the stock or water and bring to the boil. Lower the heat and simmer for 10 minutes, then process in a blender or food processor and sieve (strain) back into the pan.

2 Crush the garlic with 5ml/1 tsp salt, then stir in 120ml/4fl oz/½ cup hot soup. Return the mixture to the pan.

3 Meanwhile, poach the eggs in a frying pan of simmering water for about 3–4 minutes, until just set. Use a slotted spoon to remove them from the pan and transfer to a warmed plate. Trim off any untidy bits of white.

4 Bring the soup back to the boil and add seasoning. Stir in the chopped coriander leaves and remove from the heat.

5 Place the bread in six soup plates or bowls and drizzle the oil over it. Ladle in the soup and stir. Add a poached egg to each bowl and serve immediately, offering olive oil at the table so that it can be drizzled over the soup to taste.

Energy 299Kcal/1249kJ; Protein 11.6g; Carbohydrate 24.6g, of which sugars 2.8g; Fat 18g, of which saturates 3.1g; Cholesterol 190mg; Calcium 170mg; Fibre 3g; Sodium 323mg.

SWEET AND SOUR CABBAGE, BEETROOT AND TOMATO BORSCHT

THERE ARE MANY VARIATIONS OF THIS CLASSIC JEWISH SOUP, WHICH MAY BE SERVED HOT OR COLD. THIS VERSION INCLUDES PLENTIFUL AMOUNTS OF CABBAGE, TOMATOES AND POTATOES.

SERVES 6

INGREDIENTS
1 onion, chopped
1 carrot, chopped
4–6 raw or vacuum-packed (cooked, not pickled) beetroot (beets), 3–4 diced and 1–2 coarsely grated
400g/14oz can tomatoes
4–6 new potatoes, cut into bitesize pieces
1 small white cabbage, thinly sliced
1 litre/1¾ pints/4 cups vegetable stock
45ml/3 tbsp sugar
30–45ml/2–3 tbsp white wine, cider vinegar or sour salt (citric acid)
45ml/3 tbsp chopped fresh dill, plus extra to garnish
salt and ground black pepper
sour cream, to garnish
buttered rye bread, to serve

1 Put the onion, carrot, diced beetroot, tomatoes, potatoes, cabbage and stock in a large pan. Bring to the boil, reduce the heat and simmer for 30 minutes, or until the potatoes are tender.

VARIATION
To make meat borscht, place 1kg/2¼lb chopped beef in a large pan. Pour over water to cover and crumble in 1 beef stock (bouillon) cube. Bring to the boil, then reduce the heat and simmer until tender. Skim any fat from the surface, then add the vegetables and proceed as above. For Kashrut, omit the sour cream and serve with unbuttered rye bread.

2 Add the grated beetroot, sugar and wine, vinegar or sour salt to the soup and cook for 10 minutes. Taste for a good sweet-sour balance and add more sugar and/or vinegar if necessary. Season.

3 Stir the chopped dill into the soup and ladle into warmed bowls immediately. Garnish each bowl with a generous spoonful of sour cream and more dill and serve with buttered rye bread.

Energy 111Kcal/470kJ; Protein 3.2g; Carbohydrate 24.6g, of which sugars 17.8g; Fat 0.6g, of which saturates 0.1g; Cholesterol 0mg; Calcium 65mg; Fibre 3.8g; Sodium 52mg.

SUMMER VEGETABLE SOUP

THIS BRIGHTLY COLOURED, FRESH-TASTING TOMATO SOUP MAKES THE MOST OF SUMMER VEGETABLES IN SEASON. ADD LOTS OF RED AND YELLOW PEPPERS TO MAKE A SWEETER VERSION.

SERVES 4

INGREDIENTS

450g/1lb ripe plum tomatoes
225g/8oz ripe yellow tomatoes
45ml/3 tbsp olive oil
1 large onion, finely chopped
15ml/1 tbsp sun-dried tomato
   purée (paste)
225g/8oz courgettes (zucchini),
   trimmed and chopped
225g/8oz yellow courgettes, `
   trimmed and chopped
3 waxy new potatoes, diced
2 garlic cloves, crushed
about 1.2 litres/2 pints/5 cups
   vegetable stock or water
60ml/4 tbsp shredded fresh basil
50g/2oz/⅔ cup freshly grated
   (shredded) Parmesan cheese
sea salt and freshly ground
   black pepper

1 Plunge all the tomatoes in boiling water for 30 seconds, refresh in cold water, then peel and chop finely. Heat the oil in a large pan, add the onion and cook gently for about 5 minutes, stirring constantly, until softened. Stir in the sun-dried tomato purée, chopped tomatoes, courgettes, diced potatoes and garlic. Mix well and cook gently for 10 minutes, shaking the pan often.

2 Pour in the stock or water. Bring to the boil, lower the heat, half cover the pan and simmer gently for 15 minutes or until the vegetables are just tender. Add more stock or water if necessary.

3 Remove the pan from the heat and stir in the basil and half the cheese. Taste for seasoning. Serve hot, sprinkled with the remaining cheese.

Energy 243Kcal/1012kJ; Protein 10.3g; Carbohydrate 20.9g, of which sugars 12g; Fat 13.7g, of which saturates 4.1g; Cholesterol 13mg; Calcium 215mg; Fibre 1.3g, Sodium 169mg.

GREEK AUBERGINE AND COURGETTE SOUP

A FUSION OF FLAVOURS FROM THE SUNNY GREEK ISLANDS CREATES THIS FABULOUS SOUP, WHICH IS SERVED WITH TZATZIKI, THE POPULAR COMBINATION OF CUCUMBER AND CREAMY YOGURT.

SERVES 4

INGREDIENTS
    2 large aubergines (eggplant),
      roughly diced
    4 large courgettes (zucchini),
      roughly diced
    1 onion, roughly chopped
    4 garlic cloves, roughly chopped
    45ml/3 tbsp olive oil
    1.2 litres/2 pints/5 cups
      vegetable stock
    15ml/1 tbsp chopped fresh oregano
    salt and ground black pepper
    mint sprigs, to garnish
For the tzatziki
    1 cucumber
    10ml/2 tsp salt
    2 garlic cloves, crushed
    5ml/1 tsp white wine vinegar
    225g/8oz/1 cup Greek (US strained
      plain) yogurt
    small bunch of fresh mint leaves,
      chopped

1 Preheat the oven to 200°C/400°F/Gas 6. Place the aubergines and courgettes in a roasting tin (pan). Add the onion and garlic, and drizzle over the olive oil. Roast for 35 minutes, turning once, until tender and slightly charred.

2 Place half the roasted vegetables in a food processor or blender. Add the stock and process until almost smooth. Pour into a large pan and add the remaining vegetables. Bring to the boil, season and stir in the chopped oregano.

3 For the tzatziki, peel, seed and dice the cucumber. Place the flesh in a colander and sprinkle with salt. Leave for 30 minutes. Mix the garlic with the vinegar and stir into the yogurt. Pat the cucumber dry on kitchen paper and fold it into the yogurt. Season to taste and stir in the mint. Chill until required.

4 Ladle the soup into bowls and garnish with mint sprigs. Hand round the bowl of tzatziki so that your guests can add a dollop or two to their soup.

Energy 188Kcal/778kJ; Protein 6.9g; Carbohydrate 8.5g, of which sugars 7.3g; Fat 14.9g, of which saturates 4.3g; Cholesterol 0mg; Calcium 134mg; Fibre 3.6g; Sodium 1027mg.

ROAST VEGETABLE MEDLEY WITH SUN-DRIED TOMATO BREAD

WINTER MEETS SUMMER IN THIS SOUP RECIPE FOR CHUNKY ROASTED ROOTS. SERVE IT WITH BREAD BAKED WITH A HINT OF ADDED SUMMER FLAVOUR IN THE FORM OF SUN-DRIED TOMATOES.

SERVES 4

INGREDIENTS

  4 parsnips, quartered lengthways
  2 red onions, cut into thin wedges
  4 carrots, thickly sliced
  2 leeks, thickly sliced
  1 small swede (rutabaga), cut into
    bite-size pieces
  4 potatoes, cut into chunks
  60ml/4 tbsp olive oil
  few sprigs of fresh thyme
  1 garlic bulb, broken into
    cloves, unpeeled
  1 litre/1¾ pints/4 cups
    vegetable stock
  salt and ground black pepper
  fresh thyme sprigs, to garnish
For the sun-dried tomato bread
  1 ciabatta loaf (about 275g/10oz)
  75g/3oz/6 tbsp butter, softened
  1 garlic clove, crushed
  4 sun-dried tomatoes, finely chopped
  30ml/2 tbsp chopped fresh parsley

1 Preheat the oven to 200°C/400°F/ Gas 6. Cut the thick ends of the parsnip quarters into four, then place them in a large roasting tin (pan). Add the onions, carrots, leeks, swede and potatoes, and spread them in an even layer.

2 Drizzle the olive oil over the vegetables. Add the thyme sprigs and the unpeeled garlic cloves. Toss well to coat with oil and roast for about 45 minutes, until all the vegetables are tender and slightly charred.

3 Meanwhile, to make the sun-dried tomato bread, cut diagonal slits along the loaf, taking care not to cut right through it. Mix the butter with the garlic, sun-dried tomatoes and parsley. Spread the mixture into each slit, then press the bread back together. Wrap the loaf in foil and bake for 15 minutes, opening the foil for the last 5 minutes.

4 Discard the thyme from the roasted vegetables. Squeeze the garlic cloves from their skins over the vegetables.

5 Process about half the vegetables with the stock in a food processor or blender until almost smooth. Pour into a pan and add the remaining vegetables. Bring to the boil and season well with salt and black pepper.

6 Ladle the soup into bowls and garnish with fresh thyme leaves. Serve the hot bread with the soup.

Energy 511Kcal/2146kJ; Protein 13.9g; Carbohydrate 72.6g, of which sugars 18.9g; Fat 20.4g, of which saturates 10.6g; Cholesterol 40mg; Calcium 218mg; Fibre 12.1g; Sodium 521mg.

BUTTERNUT SQUASH AND BLUE CHEESE RISOTTO SOUP

THIS IS, IN FACT, A VERY WET RISOTTO, BUT IT BEARS MORE THAN A PASSING RESEMBLANCE TO SOUP AND MAKES A VERY SMART FIRST COURSE FOR A DINNER PARTY.

SERVES 4

INGREDIENTS
    25g/1oz/2 tbsp butter
    30ml/2 tbsp olive oil
    2 onions, finely chopped
    ½ celery stick, finely sliced
    1 small butternut squash, peeled,
      seeded and cut into small cubes
    15ml/1 tbsp chopped sage
    300g/11oz/1½ cups risotto rice
    1.2 litres/2 pints/5 cups hot
      vegetable stock
    30ml/2 tbsp double (heavy) cream
    115g/4oz blue cheese, finely diced
    30ml/2 tbsp olive oil
    4 large sage leaves
    salt and ground black pepper

1 Place the butter in a large pan with the oil and heat gently. Add the onions and celery, and cook for 4–5 minutes, until softened.

2 Stir in the butternut squash and cook for 3–4 minutes, then add the sage.

3 Add the rice and cook for 1–2 minutes, stirring, until the grains are slightly translucent. Add the chicken stock a ladleful at a time.

4 Cook until each ladleful of stock has been absorbed before adding the next. Continue adding the stock in this way until you have a very wet rice mixture. Season and stir in the cream.

5 Meanwhile, heat the oil in a frying pan and fry the sage leaves for a few seconds until crisp. Drain.

6 Stir the blue cheese into the risotto soup and ladle it into bowls. Garnish with a fried sage leaf.

Energy 505Kcal/2100kJ; Protein 9.2g; Carbohydrate 63.7g, of which sugars 5.7g; Fat 23g, of which saturates 8.3g; Cholesterol 26mg; Calcium 110mg; Fibre 2.7g; Sodium 91mg.

MIXED MUSHROOM SOLYANKA WITH PICKLED CUCUMBER

THE TART FLAVOURS OF PICKLED CUCUMBER, CAPERS AND LEMON ADD EXTRA BITE TO THIS TRADITIONAL RUSSIAN SOUP. THIS IS THE PERFECT DISH TO SERVE WHEN YOU WANT TO OFFER SOMETHING A LITTLE DIFFERENT.

2 Add the remaining vegetable stock with the sliced mushrooms, bring to the boil, cover and simmer gently for about 30 minutes.

3 In a small bowl, blend the tomato purée with 30ml/2 tbsp of stock.

4 Add the tomato purée to the pan with the pickled cucumber, bay leaf, capers, salt and peppercorns. Cook gently for a further 10 minutes.

5 Ladle the soup into warmed bowls and sprinkle lemon rind curls, a few olives and a sprig of flat leaf parsley over each bowl before serving.

SERVES 4

INGREDIENTS

2 onions, chopped
1.2 litres/2 pints/5 cups
  vegetable stock
450g/1lb/6 cups mushrooms, sliced
20ml/4 tsp tomato purée (paste)
1 pickled cucumber, chopped
1 bay leaf
15ml/1 tbsp capers in brine, drained
pinch of salt
6 peppercorns, crushed
lemon rind curls, green olives and
  sprigs of flat leaf parsley, to garnish

1 Put the onions in a large pan with 50ml/2fl oz/¼ cup of the stock. Cook, stirring occasionally, until all the liquid has evaporated.

COOK'S TIP

Using a mixture of mushrooms gives this soup its character. Try using varieties such as Paris Browns, field (portabello) and button (white) mushrooms.

Energy 35Kcal/147kJ; Protein 3g; Carbohydrate 4.6g, of which sugars 3.6g; Fat 0.7g, of which saturates 0.1g; Cholesterol 0mg; Calcium 20mg; Fibre 2g; Sodium 34mg

RUSSIAN SPINACH AND ROOT VEGETABLE SOUP WITH DILL

THIS IS A TYPICAL RUSSIAN SOUP, TRADITIONALLY PREPARED WHEN THE FIRST VEGETABLES OF SPRINGTIME APPEAR. EARTHY ROOT VEGETABLES, COOKED WITH FRESH SPINACH LEAVES, ARE ENLIVENED WITH A TART, FRESH TOPPING OF DILL, LEMON AND SOUR CREAM.

SERVES 4–6

INGREDIENTS

   1 small turnip, cut into chunks
   2 carrots, sliced or diced
   1 small parsnip, cut into large dice
   1 potato, peeled and diced
   1 onion, chopped or cut into chunks
   1 garlic clove, finely chopped
   ¼ celeriac bulb, diced
   1 litre/1¾ pints/4 cups vegetable
     stock
   200g/7oz spinach, washed and
     roughly chopped
   1 small bunch fresh dill, chopped
   salt and ground black pepper
For the garnish
   2 hard-boiled eggs, sliced
   1 lemon, cut into slices
   250ml/8fl oz/1 cup sour cream
   30ml/2 tbsp fresh parsley and dill

1 Put the turnip, carrots, parsnip, potato, onion, garlic, celeriac and stock into a large pan. Bring to the boil, then simmer for 25–30 minutes, or until the vegetables are very tender.

COOK'S TIP
For the best results, use a really good-quality vegetable stock.

2 Add the spinach to the pan and cook for a further 5 minutes, or until the spinach is tender but still green and leafy. Season with salt and pepper.

3 Stir the dill into the soup, then ladle into bowls and serve garnished with egg, lemon, sour cream and a sprinkling of parsley and dill.

Energy 229Kcal/952kJ; Protein 7.8g; Carbohydrate 14.3g, of which sugars 9.2g; Fat 16.2g, of which saturates 8.7g; Cholesterol 133mg; Calcium 197mg; Fibre 4.1g; Sodium 148mg.

THAI OMELETTE SOUP

THIS IS A SURPRISINGLY SATISFYING SOUP FROM THAILAND THAT IS VERY QUICK AND EASY TO PREPARE. IT IS A VERSATILE RECIPE, TOO, IN THAT YOU CAN VARY THE VEGETABLES YOU USE ACCORDING TO WHAT IS SEASONALLY AVAILABLE.

SERVES 4

INGREDIENTS

1 egg
15ml/1 tbsp groundnut (peanut) oil
900ml/1½ pints/3¾ cups
   vegetable stock
2 large carrots, finely diced
4 outer leaves Savoy
   cabbage, shredded
30ml/2 tbsp soy sauce
2.5ml/½ tsp granulated sugar
2.5ml/½ tsp ground black pepper
fresh coriander (cilantro) leaves,
   to garnish

VARIATION
Use pak choi (bok choy) instead of Savoy cabbage. In Thailand there are about forty different types of pak choi, including miniature versions.

1 Put the egg in a bowl and beat lightly with a fork. Heat the oil in a small frying pan until it is hot, but not smoking. Pour in the egg and swirl the pan so that it coats the base evenly. Cook over a medium heat until the omelette has set and the underside is golden. Slide it out of the pan and roll it up like a pancake. Slice into 5mm/¼in rounds and set aside for the garnish.

2 Put the stock into a large pan. Add the carrots and cabbage and bring to the boil. Reduce the heat and simmer for 5 minutes, then add the soy sauce, granulated sugar and pepper.

3 Stir well, then pour into warmed bowls. Lay a few omelette rounds on the surface of each portion and complete the garnish with the coriander leaves.

Energy 64Kcal/264kJ; Protein 2.3g; Carbohydrate 4.3g, of which sugars 4.1g; Fat 4.3g, of which saturates 0.7g; Cholesterol 48mg; Calcium 27mg; Fibre 1.1g; Sodium 560mg.

THAI MIXED VEGETABLE SOUP

IN THAILAND, THIS TYPE OF SOUP IS USUALLY MADE IN LARGE QUANTITIES AND THEN REHEATED FOR CONSUMPTION OVER SEVERAL DAYS. IF YOU WOULD LIKE TO DO THE SAME, DOUBLE OR TREBLE THE QUANTITIES. CHILL LEFTOVER SOUP RAPIDLY AND REHEAT THOROUGHLY BEFORE SERVING.

SERVES 4

INGREDIENTS
   30ml/2 tbsp groundnut (peanut) oil
   15ml/1 tbsp magic paste (see
      Cook's Tip)
   90g/3½oz Savoy cabbage or
      Chinese leaves (Chinese cabbage),
      finely shredded
   90g/3½oz mooli (daikon),
      finely diced
   1 medium cauliflower,
      coarsely chopped
   4 celery sticks, coarsely chopped
   1.2 litres/2 pints/5 cups
      vegetable stock
   130g/4½oz fried tofu, cut into
      2.5cm/1in cubes
   5ml/1 tsp palm sugar or light
      muscovado (brown) sugar
   45ml/3 tbsp light soy sauce

1 Heat the groundnut oil in a large, heavy pan or wok. Add the magic paste and cook over a low heat, stirring frequently, until it gives off its aroma. Add the shredded Savoy cabbage or Chinese leaves, mooli, cauliflower and celery. Pour in the vegetable stock, increase the heat to medium and bring to the boil, stirring occasionally. Gently stir in the tofu cubes.

2 Add the sugar and soy sauce. Reduce the heat and simmer for 15 minutes, until the vegetables are cooked and tender. Taste and add a little more soy sauce if needed. Serve hot.

COOK'S TIP
Magic paste is a mixture of crushed garlic, white pepper and coriander (cilantro). Look for it at Thai markets.

Energy 167Kcal/693kJ; Protein 10.4g; Carbohydrate 4.9g, of which sugars 4.2g; Fat 11.9g, of which saturates 0.8g; Cholesterol 0mg; Calcium 521mg; Fibre 1.9g; Sodium 832mg.

WILD MUSHROOM SOUP
WITH SOFT POLENTA

THIS RICH SOUP, SERVED WITH SOFT PARMESAN-ENRICHED POLENTA, PROVIDES PLENTY OF SCOPE FOR INDIVIDUAL VARIATIONS, DEPENDING ON YOUR CHOICE OF WILD MUSHROOMS.

SERVES 6

INGREDIENTS
  20g/¾oz/scant ½ cup dried
    porcini mushrooms
  175ml/6fl oz/¾ cup hot water
  50g/2oz/¼ cup butter
  1 large red onion, chopped
  3 garlic cloves, chopped
  115g/4oz/1¾ cups mixed wild
    mushrooms, trimmed
  120ml/4fl oz/½ cup light red wine
  1.2 litres/2 pints/5 cups
    vegetable stock
  2.5ml/½ tsp wholegrain mustard
  salt and ground black pepper
  chopped fresh parsley, to garnish
For the polenta
  750ml/1¼ pints/3 cups milk
  175g/6oz/1 cup quick-cook polenta
  50g/2oz/¼ cup butter
  50g/2oz/⅔ cup freshly grated
    Parmesan cheese, plus extra to serve

1 Put the dried porcini in a bowl and pour over the hot water. Leave them to soak for about 30 minutes. Drain, then strain the liquid through a fine sieve (strainer); reserve both the liquid and the mushrooms.

2 Melt the butter in a large pan. Add the onion and garlic and cook for 4–5 minutes, until softened. Add the mixed wild mushrooms and cook for a further 3–4 minutes.

3 Add the dried mushrooms and strain in the soaking liquid through a sieve (strainer) lined with muslin (cheesecloth) or a coffee filter. Pour in the wine and stock, and cook for 15 minutes or until the liquid has reduced by half. Remove from the heat and cool slightly.

4 Ladle half the soup into a food processor or blender and process until almost smooth. Pour the processed soup back into the soup remaining in the pan and set aside.

5 To make the polenta, bring the milk to the boil and pour in the polenta in a steady stream, stirring continuously. Cook for about 5 minutes, or until the polenta begins to come away from the side of the pan. Beat in the butter, then stir in the Parmesan.

6 Return the soup to the heat and bring just to the boil. Stir in the wholegrain mustard and season well.

7 Divide the polenta among six bowls and ladle the soup around it. Sprinkle over the grated Parmesan and the chopped parsley. Serve immediately.

COOK'S TIP
Many large supermarkets now sell a range of wild and cultivated mushrooms, both fresh and dried. If you can't find any, then substitute a mixture of well-flavoured cultivated varieties such as shiitake and chestnut.

GOAN POTATO SOUP <u>WITH</u> SPICED PEA SAMOSAS

IN GOA THIS SOUP WOULD BE SERVED AS A COMPLETE MEAL. BOTH SOUP AND SAMOSAS ARE SIMPLE TO PREPARE, AND MAKE A SUBSTANTIAL VEGETARIAN LUNCH.

SERVES 4

INGREDIENTS
  60ml/4 tbsp sunflower oil
  10ml/2 tsp black mustard seeds
  1 large onion, chopped
  1 red chilli, seeded and chopped
  2.5ml/½ tsp ground turmeric
  1.5ml/¼ tsp cayenne pepper
  900g/2lb potatoes, cut into cubes
  4 fresh curry leaves
  750ml/1¼ pint/3 cups water
  225g/8oz spinach leaves, torn if large
  400ml/14fl oz/1⅔ cups coconut milk
  handful of fresh coriander
    (cilantro) leaves
  salt and ground black pepper
For the samosa dough
  275g/10oz/2½ cups plain
    (all-purpose) flour
  1.5ml/¼ tsp salt
  30ml/2 tbsp sunflower oil
  150ml/¼ pint/⅔ cup warm water
For the samosa filling
  60ml/4 tbsp sunflower oil
  1 small onion, finely chopped
  175g/6oz/1½ cups frozen peas,
    thawed
  15ml/1 tbsp grated fresh root ginger
  1 green chilli, seeded and
    finely chopped
  45ml/3 tbsp water
  350g/12oz cooked potatoes,
    finely diced
  7.5ml/1½ tsp ground coriander
  5ml/1 tsp garam masala
  7.5ml/1½ tsp ground cumin
  1.5ml/¼ tsp cayenne pepper
  10ml/2 tsp lemon juice
  30ml/2 tbsp chopped fresh
    coriander
  vegetable oil, for deep frying

1 Make the samosa dough. Mix the flour and salt in a bowl and make a well in the middle. Add the oil and water and mix in the flour to make a soft dough. Knead briefly on a lightly floured surface. Wrap in clear film (plastic wrap) and chill for 30 minutes.

2 To make the filling, heat the oil in a frying pan and add the onion. Cook for 6–7 minutes until golden. Add the peas, ginger, chilli and water. Cover and simmer for 5–6 minutes, until the peas are cooked. Add the potatoes, spices and lemon juice. Cook over a low heat for 2–3 minutes. Stir in the coriander and season well. Leave to cool.

3 Divide the dough into eight. On a floured surface, roll out one piece into an 18cm/7in round. Keep the remaining dough covered. Cut the round in half and place 30ml/2 tbsp of the filling on each half towards one corner.

4 Dampen the edges and fold the dough over the filling. Pinch the edges together to form triangles. Repeat with the remaining dough and filling.

5 Heat the oil for deep frying to 190°C/375°F, or until a cube of bread rises and sizzles in 30 seconds. Fry the samosas for 4–5 minutes, turning once. Drain on kitchen paper.

6 To make the soup, heat the oil in a large pan. Add the mustard seeds, cover and cook until they begin to pop. Add the onion and chilli and cook for 5–6 minutes, until softened. Stir in the turmeric, cayenne, potatoes, curry leaves and water. Cover and cook over a low heat for 15 minutes, stirring occasionally, until the potatoes are soft.

7 Add the spinach and cook for 5 minutes. Stir in the coconut milk and cook for a further 5 minutes. Season and add the coriander leaves before ladling the soup into bowls. Serve with the vegetable samosas.

Energy 836Kcal/3503kJ; Protein 16.7g; Carbohydrate 112g, of which sugars 8.6g; Fat 38.7g, of which saturates 4.9g; Cholesterol 0mg; Calcium 227mg; Fibre 8.9g; Sodium 117mg.

LEGUME SOUPS

Soups made with legumes – peas, beans and lentils – are very
nutritious for vegetarians as they contain protein, fibre,
minerals and B vitamins, and are low in fat. For a quick and
easy lunch, try a simple Potage of Lentils or Catalan Potato
Broad Bean Soup, served with some warm crusty bread.
On special occasions, impress your guests with Thai-style
Lentil and Coconut Soup, Black-eyed Bean and Tomato Broth,
or American Red Bean Soup with Guacamole Salsa.

BROAD BEAN MINESTRONE

THE CLASSIC, WINTRY MINESTRONE SOUP TAKES ON A SUMMER-FRESH IMAGE IN THIS LIGHT RECIPE.
ANY SMALL PASTA SHAPES CAN BE USED INSTEAD OF THE SPAGHETTINI IF YOU PREFER.

SERVES 6

INGREDIENTS
30ml/2 tbsp olive oil
2 onions, peeled and finely chopped
2 garlic cloves, peeled and
finely chopped
2 carrots, very finely chopped
1 celery stick, very finely chopped
1.27 litres/2¼ pints/5⅔ cups
boiling water
450g/1lb shelled fresh broad
(fava) beans
225g/8oz mangetouts (snow peas),
cut into fine strips
3 tomatoes, peeled and chopped
5ml/1 tsp tomato purée (paste)
50g/2oz spaghettini, broken into
4cm/1½ in lengths
225g/8oz baby spinach
30ml/2 tbsp chopped fresh parsley
handful of fresh basil leaves
salt and ground black pepper
basil sprigs, to garnish
freshly grated Parmesan cheese,
to serve

1 Heat the oil in a pan and add the chopped onions and garlic. Cook over a low heat for 4–5 minutes, until softened but not browned.

2 Add the carrots and celery, and cook for 2–3 minutes. Add the boiling water and simmer for 15 minutes, until the vegetables are tender.

3 Cook the broad beans in boiling salted water for 4–5 minutes. Remove with a slotted spoon, refresh under cold water and set aside.

4 Bring the pan of water back to the boil, add the mangetouts and cook for 1 minute until just tender. Drain, then refresh under cold water and set aside.

5 Add the tomatoes and the tomato purée to the soup. Cook for 1 minute. Purée two or three large ladlefuls of the soup and a quarter of the broad beans in a food processor or blender until smooth. Set aside.

6 Add the spaghettini to the remaining soup and cook for 6–8 minutes, until tender. Stir in the purée and spinach and cook for 2–3 minutes. Add the rest of the broad beans, the mangetouts and parsley, and season well.

7 When you are ready to serve the soup, stir in the basil leaves, ladle the soup into deep cups or bowls and garnish with sprigs of basil. Serve a little grated Parmesan with the soup.

Energy 162Kcal/682kJ; Protein 9.9g; Carbohydrate 20.8g, of which sugars 6.5g; Fat 4.9g, of which saturates 0.7g; Cholesterol 0mg; Calcium 137mg; Fibre 7.9g; Sodium 72mg.

CATALAN POTATO AND BROAD BEAN SOUP

BROAD BEANS ARE ALSO KNOWN AS FAVA BEANS. WHILE THEY ARE IN SEASON, FRESH BEANS ARE IDEAL, BUT TINNED OR FROZEN WILL MAKE A PERFECTLY GOOD SUBSTITUTE.

SERVES 6

INGREDIENTS
30ml/2 tbsp olive oil
2 onions, chopped
3 large floury potatoes, diced
450g/1lb fresh broad (fava) beans
1.75 litres/3 pints/7½ cups
  vegetable stock
1 bunch coriander (cilantro),
  finely chopped
150ml/¼ pint/⅔ cup single
  (light) cream
salt and ground black pepper
fresh coriander, to garnish

COOK'S TIP
Broad (fava) beans sometimes have a tough outer skin, particularly if they are large. To remove this, first cook the beans briefly, peel off the skin, and add the tender centre part to the soup.

1 Heat the oil in a large pan and fry the onions, stirring occasionally, for about 5 minutes until softened but not brown.

2 Add the potatoes, beans (reserving a few for garnishing) and stock to the mixture in the pan and bring to the boil, then simmer for 5 minutes.

3 Stir in the coriander and simmer for a further 10 minutes.

4 Process the mixture in a blender or food processor (you may have to do this in batches) then return the soup to the pan.

5 Stir in the cream (reserving a little for garnishing). Season to taste with salt and pepper, and bring to a simmer.

6 Serve garnished with more coriander leaves, beans and cream.

Energy 187Kcal/784kJ; Protein 8.1g; Carbohydrate 19.2g, of which sugars 3.5g; Fat 9.2g, of which saturates 3.7g; Cholesterol 14mg; Calcium 89mg; Fibre 6.1g; Sodium 22mg.

American Red Bean Soup
with Guacamole Salsa

THIS SOUP IS IN TEX-MEX STYLE, AND IT IS SERVED WITH A COOLING AVOCADO AND LIME SALSA. IF YOU RELISH CHILLIES, ADD A LITTLE MORE CAYENNE FOR A TRULY FIERY EXPERIENCE.

<u>SERVES 6</u>

INGREDIENTS
   30ml/2 tbsp olive oil
   2 onions, chopped
   2 garlic cloves, chopped
   10ml/2 tsp ground cumin
   1.5ml/¼ tsp cayenne pepper
   15ml/1 tbsp paprika
   15ml/1 tbsp tomato purée (paste)
   2.5ml/½ tsp dried oregano
   400g/14oz can chopped tomatoes
   2 x 400g/14oz cans red kidney
      beans, drained and rinsed
   900ml/1½ pints/3¾ cups water
   salt and ground black pepper
   Tabasco sauce, to serve
For the guacamole salsa
   2 avocados
   1 small red onion, finely chopped
   1 green chilli, seeded and chopped
   15ml/1 tbsp chopped fresh
      coriander (cilantro)
   juice of 1 lime

1 Heat the oil in a pan and add the onions and garlic. Cook for 4–5 minutes, until softened. Add the cumin, cayenne and paprika, and cook for 1 minute.

2 Stir in the tomato purée and cook for a few seconds, then stir in the oregano. Add the chopped tomatoes, kidney beans and water. Bring to the boil and simmer for 15–20 minutes.

3 Cool the soup slightly, then purée it in a food processor or blender until smooth. Return to the pan and season.

4 To make the guacamole salsa, halve, stone (pit) and peel the avocados, then dice them finely. Place in a small bowl and gently, but thoroughly, mix with the finely chopped red onion and chilli, and the coriander and lime juice.

5 Reheat the soup and ladle into bowls. Spoon a little guacamole salsa into the middle of each and serve, offering Tabasco sauce separately.

Energy 244Kcal/1023kJ; Protein 10.5g; Carbohydrate 27.5g, of which sugars 7.4g; Fat 11g, of which saturates 2g; Cholesterol 0mg; Calcium 108mg; Fibre 10g; Sodium 535mg.

BUTTER BEAN, SUN-DRIED TOMATO AND PESTO SOUP

THIS SOUP IS SO QUICK AND EASY TO MAKE, AND USING PLENTY OF PESTO AND SUN-DRIED TOMATO PASTE GIVES IT A RICH, MINESTRONE-LIKE FLAVOUR.

SERVES 4

INGREDIENTS
- 900ml/1½ pints/3¾ cups vegetable stock
- 2 x 400g/14oz cans butter (lima) beans
- 60ml/4 tbsp sun-dried tomato purée (paste)
- 75ml/5 tbsp pesto

COOK'S TIP
Use a good-quality home-made or bought fresh stock for the best results. Vegetarians should use vegetable stock.

VARIATION
As an alternative to butter beans, use haricot (navy) or cannellini beans.

1 Drain and rinse the butter beans. Put the drained beans in a large pan with the stock and bring just to the boil.

2 Reduce the heat and stir in the tomato purée and pesto. Cover, bring back to simmering point and cook gently for 5 minutes.

3 Transfer six ladlefuls of the soup to a blender or food processor, scooping up plenty of the beans. Process until smooth, then return to the pan.

4 Heat gently, stirring frequently, for 5 minutes, then season if necessary. Ladle into four warmed soup bowls.

Energy 264Kcal/1109kJ; Protein 14.8g; Carbohydrate 27.4g, of which sugars 3.6g; Fat 11.3g, of which saturates 2.7g; Cholesterol 6mg; Calcium 109mg; Fibre 9.5g; Sodium 932mg.

Old Country Mushroom, Bean and Barley Soup

This hearty Jewish soup is perfect on a freezing cold day. Serve in warmed bowls, with plenty of rye or pumpernickel bread.

SERVES 6–8

INGREDIENTS

30–45ml/2–3 tbsp small haricot
  (navy) beans, soaked overnight
45–60ml/ 3–4 tbsp green split peas
45–60ml/3–4 tbsp yellow split peas
90–105ml/6–7 tbsp pearl barley
1 onion, chopped
2 carrots, sliced
3 celery sticks, diced or sliced
½ baking potato, peeled and cut
  into chunks
10g/¼oz or 45ml/3 tbsp mixed
  flavourful dried mushrooms
5 garlic cloves, sliced
2 litres/3½ pints/8 cups water
2 vegetable stock (bouillon) cubes
salt and ground black pepper
30–45ml/2–3 tbsp chopped fresh
  parsley, to garnish

1 In a large pan, put the beans, green and yellow split peas, pearl barley, onion, carrots, celery, potato, mushrooms, garlic and water.

2 Bring the mixture to the boil, then reduce the heat, cover and simmer gently for about 1½ hours, or until the beans are tender.

3 Crumble the stock cubes into the soup and taste for seasoning. Ladle into warmed bowls, garnish with parsley and serve with rye or pumpernickel bread.

COOK'S TIP
Do not add the stock (bouillon) cubes until the end of cooking as the salt will stop the beans from becoming tender.

Energy 171Kcal/726kJ; Protein 7.7g; Carbohydrate 35.4g, of which sugars 3.7g; Fat 0.8g, of which saturates 0.1g; Cholesterol 0mg; Calcium 37mg; Fibre 3.3g; Sodium 27mg.

TUSCAN CANNELLINI BEAN SOUP
WITH CAVOLO NERO

CAVOLO NERO IS A VERY DARK GREEN CABBAGE WITH A NUTTY FLAVOUR FROM TUSCANY AND SOUTHERN ITALY. IT IS IDEAL FOR THIS TRADITIONAL RECIPE.

SERVES 4

INGREDIENTS

    2 x 400g/14oz cans chopped
      tomatoes with herbs
    250g/9oz cavolo nero leaves, or
      Savoy cabbage
    400g/14oz can cannellini beans,
      drained and rinsed
    60ml/4 tbsp extra virgin olive oil
    salt and ground black pepper

1 Pour the tomatoes into a large pan and add a can of cold water. Season with salt and pepper and bring to the boil, then reduce the heat to a simmer.

2 Roughly shred the cabbage leaves and add them to the pan. Partially cover the pan and simmer gently for about 15 minutes, or until the cabbage is tender.

3 Add the cannellini beans to the pan and warm through for a few minutes. Check and adjust the seasoning, then ladle the soup into bowls, drizzle each one with a little olive oil and serve.

Energy 227Kcal/950kJ; Protein 8.2g; Carbohydrate 22.3g, of which sugars 10.4g; Fat 12.2g, of which saturates 1.9g; Cholesterol 0mg; Calcium 60mg; Fibre 7.9g; Sodium 443mg.

TUSCAN BEAN SOUP

THIS ITALIAN SOUP IS KNOWN AS RIBOLLITA. IT IS RATHER LIKE MINESTRONE, BUT MADE WITH BEANS INSTEAD OF PASTA, AND IS TRADITIONALLY LADLED OVER A RICH GREEN VEGETABLE, SUCH AS SPINACH.

SERVES 6

INGREDIENTS
45ml/3 tbsp olive oil
2 onions, chopped
2 carrots, sliced
4 garlic cloves, crushed
2 celery sticks, thinly sliced
1 fennel bulb, trimmed and chopped
2 large courgettes (zucchini),
  thinly sliced
400g/14oz can chopped tomatoes
30ml/2 tbsp home-made or
  bought pesto
900ml/1½ pints/3¾ cups
  vegetable stock
400g/14oz can haricot (navy) or
  borlotti beans, drained
salt and ground black pepper
For the base
15ml/1 tbsp extra virgin olive oil,
  plus extra for drizzling
450g/1lb fresh young spinach
ground black pepper

1 Heat the oil in a large pan. Add the chopped onions, carrots, crushed garlic, celery and fennel and fry gently for about 10 minutes. Add the courgettes and fry for a further 2 minutes.

2 Stir in the chopped tomatoes, pesto, stock and beans and bring to the boil. Lower the heat, cover and simmer gently for 25–30 minutes, until the vegetables are completely tender. Season with salt and black pepper to taste.

3 Heat the oil in a frying pan and fry the spinach for 2 minutes, or until wilted. Spoon the spinach into heated soup bowls, then ladle the soup over the spinach. Just before serving, drizzle with olive oil and sprinkle with ground black pepper.

VARIATION
Use other dark greens, such as chard or cabbage, instead of the spinach; simply shred and cook until tender, then ladle the soup over the top.

Energy 197Kcal/822kJ; Protein 6.8g; Carbohydrate 20.8g, of which sugars 10.3g; Fat 10.2g, of which saturates 1.5g; Cholesterol 0mg; Calcium 93mg; Fibre 7.7g; Sodium 287mg.

BEAN AND PISTOU SOUP

THIS HEARTY VEGETARIAN SOUP IS A TYPICAL PROVENÇAL-STYLE SOUP, RICHLY FLAVOURED WITH A HOME-MADE GARLIC AND FRESH BASIL PISTOU SAUCE.

SERVES 4–6

INGREDIENTS

150g/5oz/scant 1 cup dried haricot
(navy) beans, soaked overnight
150g/5oz/scant 1 cup dried flageolet
or cannellini beans, soaked overnight
1 onion, chopped
1.2 litres/2 pints/5 cups hot
vegetable stock
2 carrots, roughly chopped
225g/8oz Savoy cabbage, shredded
1 large potato, about 225g/8oz,
roughly chopped
225g/8oz French (green) beans,
chopped
salt and ground black pepper
basil leaves, to garnish
For the pistou
4 garlic cloves
8 large sprigs basil leaves
90ml/6 tbsp olive oil
60ml/4 tbsp freshly grated
Parmesan cheese

1 Soak a bean pot in cold water for 20 minutes, then drain. Drain the soaked haricot and flageolet or cannellini beans and place in the bean pot. Add the chopped onion and pour over sufficient cold water to come 5cm/2in above the beans. Cover and place the pot in an unheated oven. Set the oven to 200°C/400°F/Gas 6 and cook for about 1½ hours, or until the beans are tender.

2 Drain the beans and onions. Place half the beans and onions in a food processor or blender and process to a paste. Return the beans and paste to the bean pot. Add the vegetable stock.

3 Add the chopped carrots, shredded cabbage, chopped potato and French beans to the bean pot. Season with salt and pepper, cover and return the pot to the oven. Reduce the oven temperature to 180°C/350°F/Gas 4 and cook for 1 hour, or until all the vegetables are cooked right through.

4 Meanwhile place the garlic and basil in a mortar and pound with a pestle, then gradually beat in the oil. Stir in the grated Parmesan. Stir half the pistou into the soup and then ladle into warmed soup bowls. Top each bowl of soup with a spoonful of the remaining pistou and serve garnished with basil.

Energy 286Kcal/1214kJ; Protein 19.8g; Carbohydrate 50.9g, of which sugars 11.1g; Fat 1.8g, of which saturates 0.3g; Cholesterol 0mg; Calcium 142mg; Fibre 16.1g; Sodium 36mg.

BLACK-EYED BEAN
AND TOMATO BROTH

THIS DELICIOUS BLACK-EYED BEAN SOUP — KNOWN AS LUBIYA IN ISRAEL — IS FLAVOURED WITH TANGY LEMON AND SPECKLED WITH CHOPPED FRESH CORIANDER. IT IS IDEAL FOR SERVING AT PARTIES; SIMPLY MULTIPLY THE QUANTITIES AS REQUIRED.

SERVES 4

INGREDIENTS

175g/6oz/1 cup black-eyed
  beans (peas)
15ml/1 tbsp olive oil
2 onions, chopped
4 garlic cloves, chopped
1 medium-hot or 2–3 mild fresh
  chillies, chopped
5ml/1 tsp ground cumin
5ml/1 tsp ground turmeric
250g/9oz fresh or canned
  tomatoes, diced
600ml/1 pint/2½ cups
  vegetable stock
25g/1oz fresh coriander (cilantro)
  leaves, roughly chopped
juice of ½ lemon
pitta bread, to serve

1 Put the beans in a pan, cover with cold water, bring to the boil and cook for 5 minutes. Remove from the heat, cover and leave to stand for 2 hours. Drain the beans, return to the pan, cover with fresh cold water, then simmer for 35–40 minutes, or until the beans are tender. Drain and set aside.

2 Heat the oil in a pan, add the onions, garlic and chilli and cook for 5 minutes, or until the onion is soft. Stir in the cumin, turmeric, tomatoes, stock, half the coriander and the beans and simmer for 20–30 minutes. Stir in the lemon juice and remaining coriander and serve at once with pitta bread.

Energy 168Kcal/712kJ; Protein 10.7g; Carbohydrate 25g, of which sugars 2.3g; Fat 3.6g, of which saturates 0.6g; Cholesterol 0mg; Calcium 52mg; Fibre 4.1g; Sodium 10mg.

MOROCCAN CHICKPEA AND LENTIL SOUP WITH HONEY BUNS

THIS THICK PULSE AND VEGETABLE SOUP IS SAID TO ORIGINATE FROM A SEMOLINA GRUEL THAT THE BERBERS ATE DURING THE COLD WINTERS IN THE ATLAS MOUNTAINS. TODAY, IT IS SERVED IN RESTAURANTS AND CAFÉS AS A HEARTY SNACK WITH HONEY-SWEETENED SPICED BREAD OR BUNS.

SERVES 8

INGREDIENTS

- 30–45ml/2–3 tbsp olive oil
- 2 onions, halved and sliced
- 2.5ml/½ tsp ground ginger
- 2.5ml/½ tsp ground turmeric
- 5ml/1 tsp ground cinnamon
- pinch of saffron threads
- 2 x 400g/14oz cans chopped tomatoes
- 5–10ml/1–2 tsp caster (superfine) sugar
- 175g/6oz/¾ cup brown or green lentils, picked over and rinsed
- about 1.75 litres/3 pints/7½ cups vegetable stock, or water
- 200g/7oz/1 generous cup dried chickpeas, soaked overnight, drained and boiled until tender
- 200g/7oz/1 generous cup dried broad (fava) beans, soaked overnight, drained and boiled until tender
- small bunch of fresh coriander (cilantro), chopped
- small bunch of flat leaf parsley, chopped
- salt and ground black pepper

for the buns
- 2.5ml/½ tsp dried yeast
- 300g/11oz/1¼ cups unbleached strong white bread flour
- 15–30ml/1–2 tbsp clear honey
- 5ml/1 tsp fennel seeds
- 250ml/8fl oz/1 cup milk
- 1 egg yolk, stirred with a little milk
- salt

1 Make the buns. Dissolve the yeast in about 15ml/1 tbsp lukewarm water. Sift the flour and a pinch of salt into a bowl. Make a well in the centre and add the dissolved yeast, honey and fennel seeds. Gradually pour in the milk, using your hands to work it into the flour along with the honey and yeast, until the mixture forms a dough – if the dough becomes too sticky to handle, add more flour.

2 Turn the dough out on to a floured surface and knead well for about 10 minutes, until it is smooth and elastic. Flour the surface under the dough and cover it with a damp cloth, then leave the dough to rise until it has doubled in size.

3 Preheat the oven to 230°C/450°F/Gas 8. Grease two baking sheets. Divide the dough into 12 balls. On a floured surface, flatten the balls of dough with the palm of your hand, then place them on a baking sheet. Brush the tops of the buns with egg yolk and bake for about 15 minutes until they are risen slightly and sound hollow when tapped underneath. Transfer to a wire rack to cool.

4 To make the soup, heat the olive oil in a stockpot or large pan. Add the onions and stir for about 15 minutes, or until they are soft.

5 Add the ginger, turmeric, cinnamon, saffron, tomatoes and sugar. Stir in the lentils and pour in the stock or water. Bring to the boil, then reduce the heat, cover and simmer for about 25 minutes, or until the lentils are tender.

6 Stir in the cooked chickpeas and beans, bring back to the boil, then cover and simmer for a further 10–15 minutes. Stir in the fresh herbs and season the soup to taste. Serve piping hot, with the honey buns.

Energy 368Kcal/1558kJ; Protein 18.3g; Carbohydrate 64.9g, of which sugars 9.7g; Fat 5.7g, of which saturates 1g; Cholesterol 2mg; Calcium 172mg; Fibre 7.5g; Sodium 74mg.

NORTH AFRICAN SPICED SOUP

CLASSICALLY KNOWN AS HARIRA, THIS SOUP IS OFTEN SERVED IN THE EVENING DURING RAMADAN, THE MUSLIM RELIGIOUS FESTIVAL WHEN FOLLOWERS FAST DURING THE DAYTIME FOR A MONTH.

SERVES 6

INGREDIENTS
1 large onion, chopped
1.2 litres/2 pints/5 cups stock
5ml/1 tsp ground cinnamon
5ml/1 tsp turmeric
15ml/1 tbsp grated ginger
pinch of cayenne pepper
2 carrots, diced
2 celery sticks, diced
400g/14oz can chopped tomatoes
450g/1lb floury potatoes, diced
5 strands saffron
400g/14oz can chickpeas, drained
30ml/2 tbsp chopped fresh
  coriander (cilantro)
15ml/1 tbsp lemon juice
salt and ground black pepper
fried wedges of lemon, to serve

1 Place the chopped onion in a large pot with 300ml/½ pint/1¼ cups of the vegetable stock. Bring the mixture to the boil and simmer gently for about 10 minutes.

2 Meanwhile, mix together the cinnamon, turmeric, ginger, cayenne pepper and 30ml/2 tbsp of stock to form a paste. Stir into the onion mixture with the carrots, celery and remaining stock.

3 Bring the mixture to a boil, reduce the heat, then cover and gently simmer for 5 minutes.

4 Add the tomatoes and potatoes and simmer gently, covered, for 20 minutes. Add the saffron, chickpeas, coriander and lemon juice. Season to taste and when piping hot serve with fried wedges of lemon.

Energy 158Kcal/668kJ; Protein 7.2g; Carbohydrate 28.4g, of which sugars 7g; Fat 2.5g, of which saturates 0.4g; Cholesterol 0mg; Calcium 64mg; Fibre 5 4g; Sodium 173mg.

POTAGE of LENTILS

THIS TRADITIONAL JEWISH SOUP IS SOMETIMES KNOWN AS ESAU'S SOUP. RED LENTILS AND VEGETABLES ARE COOKED AND PURÉED, THEN SHARPENED WITH LOTS OF LEMON JUICE.

SERVES 4

INGREDIENTS
45ml/3 tbsp olive oil
1 onion, chopped
2 celery sticks, chopped
1–2 carrots, sliced
8 garlic cloves, chopped
1 potato, peeled and diced
250g/9oz/generous 1 cup red lentils,
  picked over and rinsed
1 litre/1¾ pints/4 cups
  vegetable stock
2 bay leaves
1–2 lemons, halved
2.5ml/½ tsp ground cumin, or
  to taste
cayenne pepper or Tabasco sauce,
  to taste
salt and ground black pepper
lemon slices and chopped
  fresh flat leaf parsley, to serve

1 Heat the oil in a large pan. Add the onion and cook for about 5 minutes, or until softened. Stir in the celery, carrots, half the garlic and all the potato. Cook for a few minutes until beginning to soften.

2 Add the lentils and stock to the pan and bring to the boil. Reduce the heat, cover and simmer for about 30 minutes, until the potato and lentils are tender.

3 Add the bay leaves, remaining garlic and half the lemons to the pan and cook the soup for a further 10 minutes. Remove the bay leaves. Squeeze the juice from the remaining lemons, then stir into the soup, to taste.

4 Pour the soup into a food processor or blender and process until smooth. (You may need to do this in batches.) Tip the soup back into the pan, stir in the cumin, cayenne pepper or Tabasco sauce, and season with salt and pepper.

5 Ladle the soup into bowls and top each portion with lemon slices and a sprinkling of chopped fresh flat leaf parsley.

VARIATION
On a hot day, serve this soup cold, with even more lemon juice.

Energy 330Kcal/1391kJ; Protein 16.3g; Carbohydrate 48.1g, of which sugars 4.7g; Fat 9.4g, of which saturates 1.4g; Cholesterol 0mg; Calcium 50mg; Fibre 4.5g; Sodium 44mg.

THAI-STYLE LENTIL <u>AND</u> COCONUT SOUP

HOT, SPICY AND RICHLY FLAVOURED, THIS SUBSTANTIAL SOUP IS ALMOST A MEAL IN ITSELF. IF YOU ARE REALLY HUNGRY, SERVE WITH CHUNKS OF WARMED NAAN BREAD OR THICK SLICES OF TOAST.

<u>SERVES 4</u>

INGREDIENTS
30ml/2 tbsp sunflower oil
2 red onions, finely chopped
1 bird's eye chilli, seeded and
  finely sliced
2 garlic cloves, chopped
2.5cm/1in piece fresh lemon grass,
  outer layers removed and inside
  finely sliced
200g/7oz/scant 1 cup red
  lentils, rinsed
5ml/1 tsp ground coriander
5ml/1 tsp paprika
400ml/14fl oz/1⅔ cups coconut milk
juice of 1 lime
3 spring onions (scallions), chopped
20g/¾oz/scant 1 cup fresh coriander
  (cilantro), finely chopped
salt and freshly ground black pepper

1 Heat the oil in a large pan and add the onions, chilli, garlic and lemon grass. Cook for 5 minutes or until the onions have softened but not browned, stirring occasionally.

COOK'S TIP
When using canned coconut milk, shake it before opening. This ensures that the layers of milk are well combined.

2 Add the lentils and spices. Pour in the coconut milk and 900ml/1½ pints/3¾ cups water, and stir. Bring to the boil, reduce the heat and simmer for 40–45 minutes, until the lentils are soft.

3 Pour in the lime juice and add the spring onions and coriander, reserving a little of each for the garnish. Season, ladle into bowls and garnish.

Energy 245Kcal/1034kJ; Protein 12.9g; Carbohydrate 35.8g, of which sugars 8.1g; Fat 6.6g, of which saturates 1g; Cholesterol 0mg; Calcium 75mg; Fibre 3.2g; Sodium 131mg.

SPICED LENTIL SOUP WITH PARSLEY CREAM

CRISPY SHALLOTS AND A PARSLEY CREAM TOP THIS RICH SOUP, WHICH IS INSPIRED BY THE DHALS OF INDIAN COOKING. CHUNKS OF SMOKED BACON ADD TEXTURE.

SERVES 6

INGREDIENTS
5ml/1 tsp cumin seeds
2.5ml/½ tsp coriander seeds
5ml/1 tsp ground turmeric
30ml/2 tbsp olive oil
1 onion, chopped
2 garlic cloves, chopped
1 smoked bacon hock
1.2 litres/2 pints/5 cups
  vegetable stock
275g/10oz/1¼ cups red lentils
400g/14oz can chopped tomatoes
15ml/1 tbsp vegetable oil
3 shallots, thinly sliced
For the parsley cream
45ml/3 tbsp chopped
  fresh parsley
150ml/¼ pint/⅔ cup Greek
  (US strained plain) yogurt
salt and ground black pepper

1 Heat a frying pan and add the cumin and coriander seeds. Roast them over a high heat for a few seconds, shaking the pan until they smell aromatic. Transfer to a mortar and crush using a pestle. Mix in the turmeric. Set aside.

2 Heat the oil in a large pan. Add the onion and garlic and cook for 4–5 minutes, until softened.

3 Add the spice mixture and cook for 2 minutes, stirring continuously.

COOK'S TIP
Tip lentils into a sieve (strainer) or colander and pick them over to remove any pieces of grit before rinsing.

4 Place the bacon in the pan and pour in the stock. Bring to the boil, cover and simmer gently for 30 minutes.

5 Add the red lentils and cook for 20 minutes or until the lentils and bacon hock are tender. Stir in the tomatoes and cook for a further 5 minutes.

6 Remove the bacon from the pan and set it aside until cool enough to handle. Leave the soup to cool slightly, then process in a food processor or blender until almost smooth. Return the soup to the rinsed-out pan. Cut the meat from the hock, discarding skin and fat, then stir it into the soup and reheat.

7 Heat the oil in a frying pan and fry the shallots for 10 minutes until crisp and golden. Remove using a slotted spoon and drain on kitchen paper.

8 To make the parsley cream, stir the chopped parsley into the yogurt and season well. Ladle the soup into bowls and add a dollop of the parsley cream to each. Pile some crisp shallots on to each portion and serve at once.

Energy 235Kcal/991kJ; Protein 13g; Carbohydrate 28.4g, of which sugars 3.7g; Fat 8.8g, of which saturates 2.2g; Cholesterol 0mg; Calcium 66mg; Fibre 2.9g; Sodium 40mg.

PASTA AND NOODLE SOUPS

In Italy hearty pasta soups are often served with bread for a light supper. There are hundreds of little pasta shapes, called pastina, to choose from — which means an endless variety of dishes is possible. In this section you will also find a tomato soup made with Israeli couscous — a toasted round pasta that is larger than regular couscous. Noodles are a key ingredient in many Asian soups. Why not try Udon Noodles with Egg Broth and Ginger, or Thai Cellophane Noodle Soup.

BORLOTTI BEAN AND PASTA SOUP

A COMPLETE MEAL IN A BOWL, THIS IS A VERSION OF A CLASSIC ITALIAN SOUP. TRADITIONALLY, THE PERSON WHO FINDS THE BAY LEAF IS HONOURED WITH A KISS FROM THE COOK.

SERVES 4

INGREDIENTS

1 onion, chopped
1 celery stick, chopped
2 carrots, chopped
75ml/5 tbsp olive oil
1 bay leaf
1 glass white wine (optional)
1 litre/1¾ pints/4 cups
  vegetable stock
400g/14oz can chopped tomatoes
300ml/½ pint/1¼ cups passata
  (bottled strained tomatoes)
175g/6oz/1½ cups dried pasta shapes,
  such as farfalle or conchiglie
400g/14oz can borlotti
  beans, drained
salt and ground black pepper
250g/9oz spinach, washed
  and drained
50g/2oz/⅔ cup freshly grated
  (shredded) Parmesan cheese, to serve

VARIATION
Other pulses, such as cannellini beans, haricot (navy) beans or chickpeas, are equally good in this soup.

1 Place the chopped onion, celery and carrots in a large pan with the olive oil. Cook over a medium heat for 5 minutes or until the vegetables soften, stirring occasionally.

2 Add the bay leaf, wine, vegetable stock, tomatoes and passata, and bring to the boil. Lower the heat and simmer for 10 minutes until the vegetables are just tender.

3 Add the pasta and beans, and bring the soup back to the boil, then simmer for 8 minutes until the pasta is *al dente*. Stir frequently to prevent the pasta from sticking.

4 Season to taste with salt and pepper. Remove any thick stalks from the spinach and add it to the mixture. Cook for a further 2 minutes. Serve in heated soup bowls sprinkled with the freshly grated Parmesan.

VARIATIONS
• This soup is also delicious with chunks of cooked spicy sausage or pieces of crispy cooked pancetta or bacon – simply add to the soup at the end of Step 3 and stir in, ensuring that the meat is piping hot before serving.
• For vegetarians, you could use fried chunks of smoked or marinated tofu as an alternative to meat.

Energy 488Kcal/2049kJ; Protein 20.5g; Carbohydrate 59.8g, of which sugars 14.1g; Fat 20.1g, of which saturates 4.9g; Cholesterol 13mg; Calcium 366mg; Fibre 11.1g; Sodium 808mg.

PASTA, BEAN AND VEGETABLE SOUP

THIS IS A CALABRIAN SPECIALITY KNOWN AS MILLECOSEDDE. THE NAME COMES FROM THE ITALIAN WORD MILLECOSE, MEANING "A THOUSAND THINGS". LITERALLY ANYTHING EDIBLE CAN GO IN THIS SOUP.

SERVES 4-6

INGREDIENTS

75g/3oz/scant ½ cup brown lentils
15g/½oz dried mushrooms
60ml/4 tbsp olive oil
1 carrot, diced
1 celery stick, diced
1 onion, finely chopped
1 garlic clove, finely chopped
a little chopped fresh flat leaf parsley
a good pinch of crushed red chillies (optional)
1.5 litres/2½ pints/6¼ cups vegetable stock
150g/5oz/scant 1 cup each canned red kidney beans, cannellini beans and chickpeas, rinsed and drained
115g/4oz/1 cup dried small pasta shapes, such as rigatoni, penne or penne rigate
salt and ground black pepper
freshly grated Pecorino cheese, to serve
chopped flat leaf parsley, to garnish

1 Put the lentils in a medium pan, add 475ml/16fl oz/2 cups water and bring to the boil over a high heat. Lower the heat to a gentle simmer and cook, stirring occasionally, for 15–20 minutes or until the lentils are just tender. Meanwhile, soak the dried mushrooms in 175ml/6fl oz/¾ cup warm water for 15–20 minutes.

2 Put the lentils in a sieve (strainer) to drain, then rinse under the cold tap. Drain the soaked mushrooms and reserve the soaking liquid. Finely chop the mushrooms and set aside.

3 Heat the oil in a large pan and add the carrot, celery, onion, garlic, parsley and chillies, if using. Cook over a low heat, stirring constantly, for 5–7 minutes, until the vegetables are soft.

4 Add the stock, then the mushrooms and their soaking liquid. Bring to the boil, then add the beans, chickpeas and lentils. Season to taste. Cover, and simmer gently for 20 minutes.

5 Add the pasta and bring back to the boil, stirring. Simmer for 7–8 minutes, until the pasta is *al dente*. Season, then serve hot in soup bowls, with grated Pecorino and chopped parsley.

COOK'S TIP
You can freeze the soup at the end of Step 4. Thaw and bring to the boil, add the pasta and simmer until tender.

Energy 668Kcal/2831kJ; Protein 41.4g; Carbohydrate 100.8g, of which sugars 7.5g; Fat 14g, of which saturates 2g; Cholesterol 0mg; Calcium 178mg; Fibre 26.1g; Sodium 44mg.

TOMATO SOUP <u>WITH</u> ISRAELI COUSCOUS

NEWLY POPULAR ISRAELI COUSCOUS IS A TOASTED, ROUND PASTA WHICH IS MUCH LARGER THAN REGULAR COUSCOUS. IT MAKES A WONDERFUL ADDITION TO THIS WARM AND COMFORTING SOUP. IF YOU LIKE YOUR SOUP REALLY GARLICKY, ADD AN EXTRA CLOVE OF CHOPPED GARLIC BEFORE SERVING.

SERVES 4–6

INGREDIENTS
  30ml/2 tbsp olive oil
  1 onion, chopped
  1–2 carrots, diced
  400g/14oz can chopped tomatoes
  6 garlic cloves, roughly chopped
  1.5 litres/2½ pints/6¼ cups
    vegetable stock
  200–250g/7–9oz/1–1½ cups
    Israeli couscous
  2–3 mint sprigs, chopped, or several
    pinches of dried mint
  1.5ml/¼ tsp ground cumin
  ¼ bunch fresh coriander (cilantro),
    or about 5 sprigs, chopped
  cayenne pepper, to taste
  salt and ground black pepper

1 Heat the oil in a large pan, add the onion and carrots and cook gently for about 10 minutes until softened. Add the tomatoes, half the garlic, stock, couscous, mint, ground cumin, coriander, and cayenne pepper, salt and pepper to taste.

2 Bring the soup to the boil, add the remaining chopped garlic, then reduce the heat slightly and simmer gently for 7–10 minutes, stirring occasionally, or until the couscous is just tender. Serve piping hot, ladled into individual serving bowls.

Energy 191Kcal/797kJ; Protein 4.2g; Carbohydrate 31.3g, of which sugars 5g; Fat 6.2g, of which saturates 0.8g; Cholesterol 0mg; Calcium 30mg; Fibre 1.4g; Sodium 44mg.

GENOESE MINESTRONE

IN GENOA, THEY OFTEN MAKE MINESTRONE LIKE THIS, WITH PESTO STIRRED IN TOWARDS THE END OF COOKING. IT IS PACKED FULL OF VEGETABLES AND HAS A STRONG, HEADY FLAVOUR, MAKING IT AN EXCELLENT VEGETARIAN SUPPER DISH WHEN SERVED WITH SOME CRUSTY BREAD.

SERVES 4

INGREDIENTS

45ml/3 tbsp olive oil
1 onion, finely chopped
2 celery sticks, finely chopped
1 large carrot, finely chopped
150g/5oz green beans, cut into
   5cm/2in pieces
1 courgette (zucchini), finely sliced
1 potato, cut into 1cm/½in cubes
¼ Savoy cabbage, shredded
1 small aubergine (eggplant), cut into
   1cm/½in cubes
200g/7oz can cannellini beans,
   drained and rinsed
2 Italian plum tomatoes, peeled
   and chopped
1.2 litres/2 pints/5 cups
   vegetable stock
90g/3½ oz spaghetti or vermicelli
salt and ground black pepper
For the pesto
   about 20 fresh basil leaves
   1 garlic clove
   10ml/2 tsp pine nuts
   15ml/1 tbsp freshly grated Parmesan
     cheese
   15ml/1 tbsp freshly grated pecorino
     cheese
   30ml/2 tbsp olive oil

1 Heat the oil in a large pan, add the chopped onion, celery and carrot, and cook over a low heat, stirring frequently, for 5–7 minutes.

2 Mix in the green beans, courgettes, potato and Savoy cabbage. Stir-fry over a medium heat for about 3 minutes. Add the aubergine, cannellini beans and plum tomatoes and stir-fry for 2–3 minutes.

3 Pour in the stock with salt and pepper to taste. Bring to the boil. Stir well, cover and lower the heat. Simmer for 40 minutes, stirring occasionally.

4 Meanwhile, process all the pesto ingredients in a food processor until the mixture forms a smooth sauce, adding 15–45ml/1–3 tbsp water through the feeder tube if the sauce is too thick.

5 Break the pasta into small pieces and add it to the soup. Simmer for 5 minutes. Stir in the pesto sauce and simmer for 2–3 minutes more, until the pasta is *al dente*. Serve hot.

COOK'S TIP
Making your own pesto gives the soup a superior flavour, but if you are short of time, ready-made bought pesto can be used instead.

VARIATIONS
Use other types of soup paste instead of spaghetti or vermicelli, if you like.

Energy 143Kcal/598kJ; Protein 4.9g; Carbohydrate 28.3g, of which sugars 5.6g; Fat 1.1g, of which saturates 0.1g; Cholesterol 0mg; Calcium 137mg; Fibre 0.6g; Sodium 362mg.

UDON NOODLES <u>WITH</u> EGG BROTH <u>AND</u> GINGER

IN THIS DISH, CALLED ANKAKE UDON, THE SOUP FOR THE UDON IS THICKENED WITH CORNFLOUR AND RETAINS ITS HEAT FOR A LONG TIME. A PERFECT LUNCH FOR A FREEZING COLD DAY.

2 Heat at least 2 litres/3½ pints/9 cups water in a large pan, and cook the udon for 8 minutes or according to the packet instructions. Drain under cold running water and wash off the starch with your hands. Leave in the sieve (strainer).

3 Pour the soup into a large pan and bring to the boil. Blend the cornflour with 60ml/4 tbsp water. Reduce the heat to medium and gradually add the cornflour mixture to the hot soup. Stir constantly. The soup will thicken after a few minutes. Reduce the heat to low.

4 Mix the egg, mustard and cress, and spring onions in a small bowl. Stir the soup once again to create a whirlpool. Pour the eggs slowly into the soup pan.

5 Reheat the udon with hot water from a kettle. Divide among four bowls and pour the soup over the top. Garnish with the ginger and serve hot.

SERVES 4

INGREDIENTS
  400g/14oz dried udon noodles
  30ml/2 tbsp cornflour (cornstarch)
  4 eggs, beaten
  50g/2oz mustard and cress
  2 spring onions (scallions),
    finely chopped
  2.5cm/1in fresh root ginger, peeled
    and finely grated, to garnish
For the soup
  1 litre/1¾ pints/4 cups water
  40g/1½oz kezuri-bushi
  25ml/1½ tbsp mirin
  25ml/1½ tbsp Japanese soy
    sauce (shoyu)
  7.5ml/1½ tsp salt

1 To make the soup, place the water and the soup ingredients in a pan and bring to the boil on a medium heat. Remove from the heat when it starts boiling. Stand for 1 minute, then strain through muslin (cheesecloth). Check the taste and add more salt if required.

COOK'S TIPS
• You can use ready-made noodle soup, available from Japanese food stores.
• Kezuri-bushi, or shaved, dried fish, is available in various graded packets.

Energy 487Kcal/2038kJ; Protein 15.5g; Carbohydrate 92.8g, of which sugars 0.6g; Fat 6.1g, of which saturates 1.6g; Cholesterol 190mg; Calcium 61mg; Fibre 0.2g; Sodium 1359mg

JAPANESE-STYLE NOODLE SOUP

THIS DELICATE, FRAGRANT SOUP IS FLAVOURED WITH JUST A SUBTLE HINT OF CHILLI. IT IS BEST SERVED AS A LIGHT LUNCH OR FIRST COURSE.

SERVES 4

INGREDIENTS
45ml/3 tbsp mugi miso
200g/7oz/scant 2 cups udon noodles,
    soba noodles or Chinese noodles
30ml/2 tbsp sake or dry sherry
15ml/1 tbsp rice or wine vinegar
45ml/3 tbsp Japanese soy sauce
115g/4oz asparagus tips or
    mangetouts (snow peas), thinly
    sliced diagonally
50g/2oz/scant 1 cup shiitake
    mushrooms, stalks removed and
    thinly sliced
1 carrot, sliced into julienne strips
3 spring onions (scallions), thinly
    sliced diagonally
salt and freshly ground black pepper
5ml/1 tsp dried chilli flakes, to serve

1 Bring 1 litre/1¾ pints/4 cups water to the boil in a pan. Pour 150ml/¼ pint/ ⅔ cup boiling water over the miso and stir until dissolved, then set aside.

2 Meanwhile, bring another large pan of lightly salted water to the boil, add the noodles and cook until just tender.

3 Drain the noodles in a colander. Rinse under cold running water, then drain again. Set aside.

COOK'S TIPS
• Mugi miso is the fermented paste of soybeans and barley.
• If fresh shiitake mushrooms are not available, use dried ones instead. Put them in a bowl, pour over boiling water and leave to stand for 30 minutes.

4 Add the sake or sherry, rice or wine vinegar and soy sauce to the pan of boiling water. Boil gently for 3 minutes or until the alcohol has evaporated, then reduce the heat and stir in the miso mixture.

5 Add the asparagus or mangetouts, mushrooms, carrot and spring onions, and simmer for 2 minutes until the vegetables are tender. Season to taste.

6 Divide the noodles among four warm bowls and pour the soup over the top. Sprinkle with the chilli flakes to serve.

Energy 220Kcal/929kJ; Protein 7.9g; Carbohydrate 39.7g, of which sugars 4.4g; Fat 4.3g, of which saturates 1.2g; Cholesterol 15mg; Calcium 37mg; Fibre 2.8g; Sodium 898mg.

THAI CELLOPHANE NOODLE SOUP

THE THAI NOODLES USED IN THIS SOUP GO BY VARIOUS NAMES: GLASS NOODLES, CELLOPHANE NOODLES, BEAN THREAD OR TRANSPARENT NOODLES. THEY ARE MADE FROM MUNG BEAN FLOUR, AND ARE ESPECIALLY VALUED FOR THEIR BRITTLE TEXTURE.

SERVES 4

INGREDIENTS

    4 large dried shiitake mushrooms
    15g/½oz dried lily buds
    ½ cucumber, coarsely chopped
    2 garlic cloves, halved
    90g/3½oz white cabbage, chopped
    1.2 litres/2 pints/5 cups boiling water
    115g/4oz cellophane noodles
    30ml/2 tbsp soy sauce
    15ml/1 tbsp palm sugar or light
      muscovado (brown) sugar
    90g/3½oz block silken tofu, diced
    fresh coriander (cilantro), to garnish

1 Soak the shiitake mushrooms and dried lily buds in two separate bowls of warm water for 30 minutes.

COOK'S TIP
Dried lily buds are the unopened flowers of day lilies. They must always be soaked in warm water before use.

2 Meanwhile, put the chopped cucumber, garlic and cabbage in a food processor or blender and process to a smooth paste. Scrape the mixture into a large pan and add the measured boiling water.

3 Bring to the boil, then reduce the heat and cook for 2 minutes, stirring the mixture occasionally. Strain this warm stock into another pan, return to a low heat and gently bring to simmering point.

4 Drain the soaked lily buds, rinse under cold running water, then drain again. Cut off any hard ends. Add the lily buds to the stock with the noodles, soy sauce and sugar and cook for 5 minutes more.

5 Strain the liquid from the soaked mushrooms into the soup. Discard the mushroom stems, then slice the caps. Divide them and the tofu among four bowls. Pour the soup over, garnish with fresh coriander leaves and serve.

Energy 143Kcal/598kJ; Protein 4.9g; Carbohydrate 28.3g, of which sugars 5.6g; Fat 1.1g, of which saturates 0.1g; Cholesterol 0mg; Calcium 137mg; Fibre 0.6g; Sodium 362mg.

INDEX